VICTORIA BATHS:
MANCHESTER'S WATER
PALACE

VICTORIA BATHS: MANCHESTER'S WATER PALACE

Prue Williams

**WITH A FOREWORD BY
GRIFF RHYS JONES**

Spire Books Ltd

in association with the

Friends of Victoria Baths

Published by
Spire Books Ltd
PO Box 2336
Reading RG4 5WJ
www.spirebooks.com

CIP data:
A catalogue record for this book is available
from the British Library
ISBN 1-904965-01-6

Designed and produced by John Elliott
Cover illustration by Colin G. Piggott
Text set in Adobe Bembo

Printed by Alden Group Ltd
Osney Mead
Oxford OX2 0EF

Contents

FOREWORD

I think it was probably the coldest day I ever spent. It felt like the coldest room I'd ever been in. You could have safely kept a few beef carcasses hanging there for a couple of months. I didn't dare sit on the marble seat. I worried I might freeze to it and get back up with a horrible tearing sound. I remember we piled six or seven coats up and I sat gingerly on them and I could still feel the fingers of ice reaching up from my bottom. I was the princess and the frozen peas, trying to present my piece to camera, in the hot room of the Victoria Baths.

It is just one reason that I am delighted that Victoria Baths won *Restoration* in 2003. The money will go to getting those freezing steam baths back into action. (Remember the Liverpool man who was fascinated by the vacuum flask. 'What a clever idea. It keeps things hot and it keeps things cold? But how does it know?') The others are numerous. Beyond the gorgeous simplicity of those rooms is a fantasy swimming pool. Oh, the changing huts with their swing doors! (I once put on a revue with a row of bathing huts which the actors emerged from in different costumes to play the sketches. They have such happy memories for everybody.) Oh, the wonderful trussed roof with its sky-lights! Oh, the mosaics! With the dolphins. Oh, the upper balcony! Oh, yes it can be a very cold place to visit in the middle of winter, but even when the only steam is on your breath and the only water in the place is leaking through the guttering and spoiling the roofs, the pools are enchanting and exhilarating.

Everybody thought that. From the moment it appeared, as the first building on the first programme of the first series, there was clearly an excitement about the idea of this 'nineteenth-century sanitary facility', as Roy Hattersley ungraciously called it. Some other candidates on the programme (Roy Hattersley) were jealous of its primary position. 'They have pushed themselves to the front of the queue,' they wailed, perhaps unconsciously remembering their own Saturday mornings with a towel roll in a tight sausage around their trunks at the turnstile. But the baths being first, they might just as easily have been the soonest forgotten. They weren't.

Everywhere I went, in taxis, at parties, once, a little disturbingly, in a police station, anxious passers-by enquired after the Victoria Baths, the belle of the programme, perhaps because they were selfish. Perhaps they liked the practicality of restoring somewhere they could amuse themselves. They liked the idea of plunging in and wallowing in the winner, diving into the victor, sharing its success with a couple of lengths. Perhaps it was because they felt, as I do, that there is something deeply resonant in our British

FOREWORD

souls about the feel of those Edwardian public baths. They were the first big swimming pools to be built. They provided a template. The designers had to use their imaginations and ingenuity. And it is that sense of discovery and invention which we admire, in an age when so much other architecture was pastiche. And so many of the municipal buildings from that era, the park houses, the pools, the theatres, the promenades and lidos, built with vast amounts of confidence and even vaster amounts of loot, often in the name of delightful and unhurried public leisure, are going, or gone already; to be replaced by our age of curtains-drawn entertainment in front of flickering lights of doom. Of course, Victoria Baths benefited from being in Manchester. There's a new ferocious pride around this town. The town got up and voted. That made the difference.

It was a pleasure to meet Gill and Sonny Lowry and all the supporters. They are working so hard to make this place succeed. Many think that, because it won, the swimming pool must be already up and running. But there is a long way to go. It is an expensive project. *Restoration* provided a mighty chunk of money but less than a third of the total.

I worked here for Red Productions last year and stayed a few weeks in the centre of town. You can see there's a lot of cash going into the redevelopment of Manchester. It fairly buzzes with scaffolders. But does it need another pool? Well, I went for a swim in the new and magnificent Commonwealth Baths. It was early evening. Half of the place was roped off for training. In order to swim my lengths I had to join a stream of swimmers, like a motorway, glide into my lane and go round and round in strict circulation. If I went too fast, I bumped into the swimmer in front; too slow and felt a thrashing at the soles of my feet. I felt like an aquatic hamster.

Earlier in the year I went to Budapest, a thermal town with pools built by the Romans and the Turks, and made a pilgrimage to the Secessionist splendours of the Gellért baths, built under the Austro-Hungarian Empire. Built at the same time as Victoria Baths, with massive rune-decorated pillars and Art Nouveau Magyar heads, it was a swimming pool out of the Abominable Dr Phibes. A treat to visit. A tourist attraction. An asset. This was Hungary, by the way – not the richest of countries.

So come on Manchester, put your money on the table. You have a treasure. Put some of your vast redevelopment loot into your heritage. It was part of your Golden Age and should undoubtedly be protected and preserved. Are there more votes in this sort of thing? Votes for politicians. We should make sure there are.

If you want to raise a million pounds, that means a thousand a day every day for three years. Think how long it takes you to earn a thousand, and you are working, at least some of the time. Victoria Baths needs more than goodwill. It needs redoubled efforts to muster cash. Big sponsors, big donors, big noise. Thank you for buying this book. Because every little helps. Victoria Baths was a very worthy winner of *Restoration*. Now we need to finish the job.

Griff Rhys Jones

ACKNOWLEDGEMENTS

I am indebted to so many people for sharing their interest in, and happy memories of, High Street Baths with me. All who swam, dived, danced, had their weekly 'real' bath there, enjoyed the occasional luxury of the Turkish baths, sauna and Aeratone, brought their weekly wash here; all had stories to tell.

I thank Beatrice Ramsden for her lovely story of romance which started at Victoria Dance Nights; Mary Eastwood for her heartfelt recollection of her father's heroism in World War I; Mrs Renée Diaz, who spent many Wednesday afternoons talking to May Flanaghan (now 99) so that she could pass on May's wonderful stories of the High Street Wash-house to me; May Flanaghan for sharing her stories; Gweneth Fitton for her letters, phone calls and visits to tell me of her mother's memories of Ellison's and to give me photographs of her grandfather and father; Zilpha Wheelton, 'the stylish Miss Zilpha Grant' as the press called her, for her letters and phone calls; Barbara Gordon, who wrote and phoned on several occasions to tell me about Arthur Howarth's long career, over 30 years at High Street Baths; Erica Rigby and Carol Iveson, née Chesworth, who wrote, phoned and visited to bring cherished memorabilia and photographs of their mother, Erica Bury (Chesworth) and also the story of her career. These items will form part of a permanent display at the Baths once the restoration work is complete; Mrs Elizabeth Ridyard wrote of her mother's memories of Mr Derbyshire, Superintendent, and Lizzie Derbyshire (her great-uncle and aunt) living at High Street Baths; Doreen Thompson, for letters and many phone calls about her memories of visiting her friend Jean Botham, at the Superintendent's flat, also for photographs; Mrs Betty Shelley for her vivid memories and description of the office and boardroom at Ellison & Co. Ltd ; Joan Gardiner, Press Officer and past President of Manchester Swimming and Water Polo Association, for her help and information on Margery Hinton.

Now I must express my thanks and deep gratitude to Sunny Lowry, our Channel swimmer, for her friendship and support, for her dedication towards saving the Baths by fund-raising and publicity. On a personal note, I was thrilled when Sunny asked me to accompany her on the BBC-sponsored journey and overnight stay in London, to take part in the *Restoration* programme. It was an unforgettable

ACKNOWLEDGEMENTS

experience made especially memorable when we received H.R.H. Prince Charles's message of congratulation and pleasure in our success. We all thank His Royal Highness for his interest and his subsequent visit to view our Victoria Baths.

I thank Phil Moss for his generous support and for allowing me to use quotes from his book *True Romances at Manchester Dances*. I am indebted to Gary James, Manchester City Football Club's Archivist and Heritage Centre Project Manager, who, despite being under great pressure due to the move from Maine Road to the new City of Manchester Stadium, found time to write a very informative letter and told me to phone for more information on City's Ellison turnstiles. Gary James's enthusiasm for the history of his club and its turnstiles is inspiring and I am very grateful for his help. I must also thank Mr John Leigh who worked for Sir W. H. Bailey's Albion Works and wrote several letters detailing much appreciated information on the manufacture of turnstiles; Reg Redfearn for sending information on his mother's, Mrs Eleanor Redfearn, career at Victoria Baths as a swimming teacher; Ian McRae, who kindly allowed me to recount his story of the Aeratone (near disaster); Mr Jack Turner for all his help, detailing his busy days of engineering work at the Baths, to ensure the smooth running of boilers, calorifiers and all the connecting pipe work; Mr Arthur Howarth for his interesting stories of his long career as a swimming teacher at High Street Baths; Mr Harry Hitchin; the last Superintendent here before the Baths were closed and Mrs Iris Hitchin, their letters, phone calls and visits gave me a very clear picture of what it was like, living and working in such a responsible position at Victoria Baths; Albert Smith, who wrote and phoned about the two great loves in his life, dancing to Big Band music and meeting his wife, Eleanor at High Street Dance Nights; Ernie Ivor Derbyshire, whose memories of his grandfather, the first Superintendent of Victoria Baths, are part of his family history; Donald Muirhead, who describes his training years at Victoria Baths as the happiest time of his life; Neil Bonner, Treasurer of the Friends of Victoria Baths and regular tour guide on Open Days, for his vivid description of the Wash-house routine; Dr Ian Gordon for letting me use quotes from his notes on so many of the national, international and Olympic swimming events; to Lawrence Burton for his letters and for allowing me to use extracts from his article on William Burton, his great-uncle; to Joyce Leah for her information on the achievements of her great-uncle William Pointer, as a stained glass maker, who made the lovely windows at the Baths; to Simon Inglis for his very informative emails on W. T. Ellison's turnstiles; Alison Kershaw for her memories of the Turkish Baths ; to Margaret Jump for the lovely story of her father, Harry Williams, and her mother, Hilda, both very much part of High Street Baths history, and Elizabeth Grayson for her letter enthusing on her enjoyment of using the Turkish Baths; and to Malcolm Shifrin for detailed information on the history of the Turkish Baths in Britain and his continued enthusiasm in promoting Turkish Baths.

We are particularly grateful to those people who agreed to be interviewed as part of our Oral History project – Derek Johnston, Nancy Dudley, Sunny Lowry, Arthur Howarth, Joe Beaumont, Phyllis Walters, Barbara Cooper and Irene Stanley. There are many other people who have shared their memories of Victoria Baths and whose notes fill our Memories File.

ACKNOWLEDGEMENTS

I thank all these people for their patience and interest. Their stories have put flesh on the bare bones of history.

I am deeply grateful to the staff at Manchester Central Library Local Studies Department for their help in the search for the necessary books, documents and maps, and also wish to thank the Tiles and Architectural Ceramics Society, and the Pilkington's Lancastrian Pottery Society for their assistance in researching our tiles, and Manchester City Council Leisure Department for photographs of Victoria Baths. I thank Barbara Neff for her typing and also my near neighbour and friend Jean Glennon who used her skill and patience to type and amend my work.

Many thanks to the Computerised Image Collection at Manchester Archives and Local Studies for permission to use many of their photographs of Victoria Baths.

Thanks also to my friends at Victoria Baths for all their help and encouragement, especially to Gill Wright and Chandy Coverley.

I thank my family, especially Pat and Alan, for putting up with my obsession with High Street Baths.

Prue Williams
May 2004

Sunny Lowry (left) and Prue Williams at Manchester Piccadilly station after returning from London the day after winning the BBC *Restoration* final (Monday 15th September 2003).

Prue Williams was born in Ipswich where she developed a love of history and old buildings. Her father's work took the family to Belgium and they lived first in Antwerp, then Genval, near Brussels. Her training to become a teacher in Antwerp was interrupted by the coming of war and, in May 1940, the family made a perilous, nine-day journey to Calais along roads clogged with refugees. They boarded HMS *Venomous* and were perhaps the only civilian family to take part in the Dunkirk evacuation!

Inspired by the calm efficiency and bravery of the crew on the destroyer, she decided to join the W.R.N.S., and, while serving, married her husband, Bill. Soon after D-Day she was 'released to shore' (the Navy's expression for discharge) due to pregnancy.

Prue, Bill and their sons Trevor and Alan moved to a house in Moss Side and Prue was captivated by Manchester. She began a full-time teaching career in 1961 but still managed to pursue interests in local history and archaeology.

She visited Victoria Baths on an Open Day in 1998, fell in love with the building, and decided to write what has become the present book.

INTRODUCTION

When, in 1998, I first set eyes on Victoria Baths, or High Street Baths as people used to call it, I couldn't believe that such a gem of Edwardian architecture and history would be in danger of demolition. Sadly, however, this proved to be the case. Had it not been for the enthusiasm and hard work of a group of dedicated volunteers, this wonderful building would have disappeared into a heap of rubble to be replaced probably by yet another office block. Already, after some six years of closure, the building had deteriorated. Attacks by vandals, pigeons and weather had damaged the beautiful stained glass windows, the roof, and the steelwork, but hopefully not beyond repair. Thanks to the skill and dedication of the original builders, the inspired planning of the City Architect, Mr Henry Price, and the aims of the City Councillors who, with marvellous foresight, were prepared to spend what was then an enormous amount of money, over £56,000, there was created in 1906 what the Lord Mayor, J. Herbert Thewliss, described as '… this Water Palace of which every citizen of Manchester will be justly proud'.

And so it has proved to be. There is so much left to admire in this wonderful building; the magnificent woodwork of the balustrades, the deep green top-quality ceramic tiling, the mosaic floors with intricate fish and sea flora patterns, the light and airiness of the three pool-halls and the many interesting facilities. There were porcelain baths in private cubicles where people could luxuriate in a weekly 'real bath', the Turkish and Russian baths and the later improvements of the Sun Ray Department and the forerunner of the Jacuzzi, the 'Aeratone'. This was described in a recent T.V. item as an 'instrument of torture' and it certainly looks the part! But that it was not. In fact it was so popular that there was always a long waiting list of people wanting to use this facility.

As well as setting out in 1993 to save the building for public use, the Friends of Victoria Baths have, over the last few years, been researching the history of the Baths, to find out more about the background to its construction and its use over the years. We have visited libraries, examined council records and read up on related subjects. But our richest source of information has been people – those who remember the Baths in years gone by, because they swam there, bathed there, danced there, worked there or had family

INTRODUCTION

Henry Price, Manchester's first City Architect, who was responsible for overseeing the construction of Victoria Baths.

members involved in its building. We have talked to people at our Open Days, spoken by telephone or corresponded by post or email. In a few cases we have recorded interviews.

Much of our source material is therefore oral, although we have always encouraged our informants to write notes of what they remember. We have used a pro-forma 'Memory Sheet' for this purpose. Where possible we have corroborated information given to us, either from another individual or from a documentary source. But this is not always possible. The story of Victoria Baths as we present it here is written in good faith following several years of research by a number of people. We think we can say that, overall, we probably now know as much about Victoria Baths as anyone ever has. But, we are learning all the time. We welcome feedback on any of the aspects of Victoria Baths covered in this book (and any that are omitted).

Now there is much work to be done to ensure that the record of Victoria Baths is preserved and that its future will continue to provide amenities for the citizens of our burgeoning City of Manchester and its many visitors.

I am hoping that this book will help towards achieving these aims.

CHAPTER 1

MANCHESTER'S BATHS AND
WASH-HOUSES, & BUILDING VICTORIA BATHS

In 1845 a Grand Ball was held in the Manchester Royal Exchange. No doubt the ladies wore their most elegant ball-dresses and glittering jewellery, the gentlemen their more sober evening wear, relieved by a rich cravat, some wearing military or civil insignia, and probably everybody had a most enjoyable time.

But there was a serious side to all this frivolity. There had been serious outbreaks of typhus, cholera, scarlet fever and other illnesses causing many deaths, especially among the workers who had come to Manchester to find employment in the mills. Our Victorian forefathers had read the reports and the findings of the doctors and healthworkers which clearly linked the atrocious housing conditions with the

Another fund-raising event: a Grand Fancy Dress Ball held on April 29th 1845 at the Free Trade Hall to raise funds for the establishment of public baths and wash-houses in Manchester.

prevalence and rapid spread of disease so, with their usual concern, they had decided on practical ways to raise money towards improving the health and welfare of their workers. In 1841, Dr Richard Howard of the Ancoats and Ardwick Dispensary gave this stern warning.:

> Until the labouring classes are supplied with the commonest necessaries of life, relieved from their state of extreme wretchedness and destitution which habitually exists, fever and disease will continue to prevail extensively among them.[1]

It was realised that, despite the efforts of the Manchester Board of Health to encourage landlords to improve their houses, many people still lived in great misery in one small room or cellar in dark and damp conditions with little through ventilation. 'Many streets were unpaved with deep potholes into which foul water, rubbish and sewage accumulated'.[2] Added to these conditions, the uncertainty of regular wages meant that many had very little in the way of furniture; a table, a stool or two, a mattress with rags for coverings in which the whole family slept, a few, very few, kitchen utensils made up the total of their possessions. It was almost impossible to keep themselves or their belongings clean, so it was small wonder that disease flourished and epidemics occurred.

In 1835 there were many deaths in Manchester from cholera. Little Ireland was a black spot; low-lying, often flooded by the River Medlock, damp and dark, the people living there in a continuous state of misery had no resistance when fevers struck. In Ancoats there were so many victims of the cholera in 1835, that Dr Schofield, a philanthropist who treated the poor free, used the garden of his house, the Roundhouse, to bury many cholera victims, including his wife and six children.

So, it was an attempt to alleviate the sad plight of the working people that brought about the Grand Ball at the Royal Exchange, which raised the magnificent sum of £440 to be used to provide public baths and laundry facilities. These were opened in April 1845 in Miller Street and furnished convenient, comfortable bathing and washing facilities for the poorer classes.[3]

The success of this project induced Sir Benjamin Heywood, a Manchester banker and member of the Statistical Society, to open a similar building in Miles Platting. He gave land and £300 towards the cost of the building, where twenty-three private baths, forty-eight washtubs and drying facilities were provided.[4]

Another curious early public baths is described in a newspaper article by Mr H. Howarth who wrote:

> The Public Baths within the rails of the Royal Infirmary [then in Piccadilly] provided a wonderful sulphurous Fumigating Baths to apply sulphur in the form of vapour. This cost 3/-. Also rooms where leeching, cupping and shampooing could be administered in comfort.

A notice warned, 'Any uncouth person who was seen to spit in the baths would be fined 1/- and

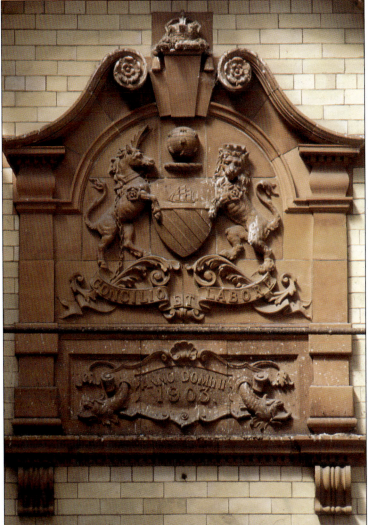

The foundation 'stone' (actually terracotta) commemorating the commencement of the construction of Victoria Baths in 1903. It bears the City Council's coat of arms and is situated in the First Class Pool.

banned from future use'. The writer comments 'Serve them right too'.[5]

Progress was slow but conditions were improving, thanks to the voluntary work of the Manchester and Salford Association, whose members undertook to visit their allotted districts regularly and to encourage people to attend illustrated lectures and to read their pamphlets written in simple language on topics such as 'Hints to working people about Personal Cleanliness'.

Thanks also to the work of Edwin Chadwick who reported on the sanitary conditions in towns to Parliament in 1844, the first Public Health Act was passed in 1848 and local Boards of Health were established. Their duty was to see that streets were swept, that houses were supplied with pure water and drainage, and that Medical Officers of Health were appointed.

In 1844 Manchester gained permission to prevent the building of any more back-to-back houses. However, the provision of houses continued for many years to be left to individual landlords, very few of whom provided bathrooms or even indoor toilets: such dwellings continued to be in use well into the 1950s. Many of our visitors to Victoria Baths speak of the luxury of having a 'real bath' there once a week.

Small wonder then that, having witnessed the improvement in the health of their citizens, many local authorities advocated a system of municipal baths and wash-houses. The Baths and Wash-Houses Act of 1846 gave local authorities the power to raise capital for the purpose of providing public bathing and washing facilities. However, for several decades up to 1876 private enterprise continued to cater for the bathing and washing facilities of the people of Manchester. The Manchester and Salford Baths and

Laundries Co. owned two establishments in Manchester – the Mayfield Baths and Wash-house, opened in 1856, and the Leaf Street facilities opened in 1860.[6]

In 1876 Manchester Corporation appointed a committee to report on the desirability of providing baths and wash-houses in the city. They agreed that a reasonable expenditure for this purpose would be a wise policy and would meet with the general approval of the ratepayers. The Mayfield and Leaf Street Baths and Wash-houses were purchased by the Corporation in 1877, and New Islington Baths were the first to be erected by the Corporation and opened to the public in 1880. During the next twenty years six further establishments were added. From the opening of Victoria Baths in 1906, hardly a year passed (except during the First World War) without a swimming baths or public wash-house, or sometimes both, being erected.

Building Victoria Baths

Imagine yourself back in time in mid-16th century Manchester. A familiar sight in the old Market Place would be a queue of women waiting their turn to collect their daily allowance of water. As the Court Leet of 1578 stated, '… in vessels of no greater capacity than one woman was able to bear and but one of every house at one turn daily'. This was because the only source of water supply at that time was a few wells and springs, the most important being that in Fountain Street. The water from here was taken by conduit to the old Market Place.

Fortunately, by the time Victoria Baths was being debated by the Manchester Council the water supply, of prime importance when considering the building of swimming baths, had greatly improved. First improvements came about when Sir Oswald Mosley, the Lord of the Manor, tapped the River Medlock near Holt Town. In 1809, these works were taken over by the Manchester and Salford Waterworks Co. With another waterworks at Gorton, a supply of 3.5 million gallons of water a day was obtained. In 1847, this company was bought out by Manchester Corporation.[7] In that same year, the Longdendale waterworks was founded, followed by Thirlmere in 1874 and Haweswater in 1913. So by the time Manchester Council first considered the provision of baths to serve the Longsight, St Luke's and Rusholme Wards in 1897, there was a plentiful supply of town water, but it was expensive.

The Committee advertised for offers of land in the district and after due consideration decided that the High Street (now Hathersage Road) site used by the Manchester Lawn Tennis Club would be the most central to the three wards. This was recommended to the Council on 28 October 1898.[8] In December 1899 terms were made with the owners and the land was purchased for £750 with the Corporation undertaking to pay the chief rents of £134 8s. 8d annually. The Council also agreed to the formation of a new street on one side of the site, the owners to give the land for the street and the Corporation to be responsible for sewering, flagging and paving. The street was later named Bax Road, after Alderman Bax.

On 7 January 1900 a Building Sub-Committee was formed with Alderman Bax as Chairman and work to put the ambitious plans forward began in earnest. The City Surveyor's Department prepared the first plans for Victoria Baths. These were approved by the Committee on 26 September and the City Surveyor was asked to prepare the necessary drawings and estimates to enable application to be made to the Local Government Board for borrowing powers. On 17 October the City Surveyor presented the following approximate estimates:

Baths	£57,000
Public Hall	£15,000
Total	£72,000

One can imagine the horror with which the worthy Councillors received this information but the Council Minutes state soberly that 'this sum was considered too much to expend'. At this time the usual cost of building baths was in the region of £12,000 to £25,000 so certain alternatives were suggested and plans for building the public hall were abandoned.

Amended plans were prepared to include three swimming baths, 64 wash baths, Turkish and Russian baths, boilers and calorifiers, caretaker's residence, etc.[9] These plans and an estimate of a probable cost of £39,998 were approved by the newly appointed City Architect, Henry Price, in 1902, and the Committee advertised for tenders. After due consideration, the tender of C. H. Normanton and Sons at £39,316 10s.0d.

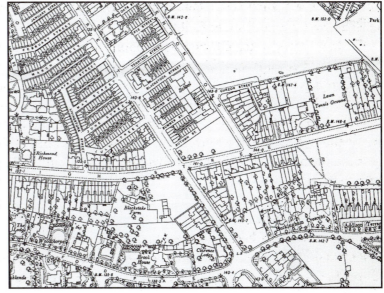

Victoria Baths was built on a site on High Street, Chorlton-on-Medlock, previously used as a Lawn Tennis Club.

Maps reproduced from the Ordnance Survey maps of 1893 (above) and 1915 (below), © Crown copyright.

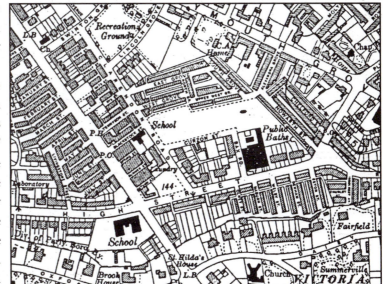

Victoria Baths made much use of terracotta. Each of the three entrances has a terracotta sign over the door.

was accepted. This was confirmed at the Council Meeting of 6 May 1903. A later comment adds '… it would perhaps have been better if it had been specifically explained to the Council that this tender was for the buildings alone'.[10]

This seems to have set the tone for the Baths Committee meetings throughout the building period. On the one hand, enthusiastic support for bigger and better baths and on the other, a more cautious approach voicing concerns about mounting costs.

The contract between Normanton and Sons and the Manchester Corporation was signed and work started. The foundation stone was laid in 1903, as commemorated on the plaque above the First Class Males pool.

The discrepancy between the original estimates and the actual costs mounted steadily as the work progressed and really concerned the Council. As we have seen, the original plans had already been amended by abandoning the public hall in order to keep within an acceptable budget. Now, after considering the expense of using town water, the Council began to favour the possible use of well water. This was not a new idea. As early as February 1900, a sub-committee, led by Alderman Bax, visited

Municipal Baths High Street. Longsight.

A postcard from the early 1900s showing Victoria Baths.

Leicester, Nottingham and, later, London. As a result of these visits, the Committee was already well informed about the advantages of using well water. It was cleaner and cheaper. There had been complaints about the colour of the town water supply in several Manchester swimming baths.

After the Baths Committee had received a letter from Councillor Beastow stating that '… from inquiries he had made he believed the geological conditions in High Street, Chorlton-on-Medlock were highly favourable to the obtaining of an abundant supply of clean water for bath purposes',[11] the Committee decided that the City Surveyor should be instructed to commence test borings at once. After initial poor results they were rewarded with a plentiful supply of water, a constant yield of over 16,000 gallons per hour and it was acknowledged by the authorities that the 'Committee acted prudently in continuing these operations.'[12]

So eventual savings would be made but the immediate costs of regular engineering work and provision of storage tanks, air lift plant, filtering and aerating plant came to an extra £4,788. This additional expenditure was not the only one as work progressed. There had not been any provision in the original scheme for a laundry, as it had been intended to do the washing of towels, etc. at the Mayfield Baths

Above: The First Class Males/Gala Pool under construction in 1905.

Right: Victoria Baths was built with both gas and electric lights.

Laundry. This had since proved impossible as that laundry was fully occupied due to New Islington Laundry having been converted to a public wash-house and their baths laundry being sent to Mayfield. As there was no room for extensions to be built at either Mayfield or New Islington, it was decided that the cheapest and best course was to provide an establishment laundry at Victoria Baths. The estimated cost was £2,100.[13]

Other alterations made by the Committee which

The Manchester Guardian, 8 September 1906.

MANCHESTER NEW BATHS OPENED BY THE LORD MAYOR

The Lord Mayor (Mr. J. Herbert Thewliss) opened two new baths yesterday in Manchester, one at Moss Side and the other – the Victoria Baths – at High-street, Chorlton-on-Medlock. Both baths have been described in the "Manchester Guardian," and it is now only necessary to say that they are probably not surpassed by the public baths of any municipality in the kingdom. The Moss Side Bath, which has been built in the centre of a new and thickly populated district, has cost nearly £13,000. The larger and more important bath in High-street has been built at a cost of £59,000.

After luncheon at the Town Hall, where Mr. Alderman Rothwell, chairman of the Baths Committee, presided, the members of the Council went first to Moss Side Baths, the main door of which the Lord Mayor opened with a gold key presented to him by the Chairman of the Committee. …

After an inspection of the buildings the members of the Corporation were driven to the Victoria Baths, where a large crowd had assembled. Here, with another gold key, the Lord Mayor opened the door, and the company passed in to the men's fine swimming bath.

In asking the Lord Mayor to declare the bath open, Mr. Alderman Rothwell said he might advance one or two considerations in justification of the action of the Baths Committee in the building of these baths. The baths were intended to serve three great wards – Longsight, Rusholme, and St. Luke's. In 1901 those wards had a population of 72,444, and he thought it might fairly be assumed that at present their population was not less than 80,000. Their rateable value at present was £392,681. The object sought to be obtained in the building of the baths had been durability and cleanliness, and with that view the best materials had been used. Under those circumstances the Committee were justified in expecting the cost in repairs and the inconvenience arising from the carrying out of those repairs would be small by comparison with other baths in the city. He had been asked whether, had it been his own business, he would have spent as much money as had been expended upon the baths. He would recommend the Baths Committee to do nothing that he would not do on his own account, and he had gone so far as to say, in answer to these criticisms, that if the Manchester City Council should happen to be dissatisfied with that institution, and should pass a resolution to the effect that it was on sale, the City Council had a purchaser to-morrow who would pay them every penny it had cost. – (Hear, hear.)

The Lord Mayor expressed the pleasure with which in the ward he represented – St. Luke's – he opened a "water palace", of which, he took it, every citizen of Manchester was proud. Speaking of the expenditure on the baths, the Lord Mayor said it was hoped to avoid the experiences of the Committee in relation to other baths in the city, where, owing to the extensive use of wood and plaster, large sums had had to be expended in alteration and repairs.

Other speeches were made by Mr. Councillor Sutton, deputy chairman of the Baths Committee, Mr. Councillor Marsden, and Mr. Councillor Scott, M.P. – who urged that swimming should be made a compulsory subject of education, – and the Lord Mayor was thanked for his attendance.

Under the direction of Mr. J. Derbyshire, general superintendent of the Corporation baths, an entertainment was afterwards given by a number of children from elementary schools, the women teachers of swimming in the employ of the Corporation, and several well-known swimmers.

drove up the costs were the use of white glazed brickwork instead of wood in the dressing boxes, bronze casements instead of wood, terrazzo and tiled floors instead of spar, and improvements to the system of electric bells:

> This brought the cost of the buildings up from the estimated £32,260 to the cost of £39,816 and that of electric lighting doubled from £500 to £1,000. The reason being that in the work then being done, all wires were placed in water-tight pipes and special provision made for protecting all fittings from damp.[14]

These were far from being the final additional expenses. There would be the cost of the wonderful stained glass windows, the polished baywood and polished pitchpine woodwork of screens, rails and balustrading, the ornamental ironwork at the turnstiles and the beautiful tiling in a variety of designs in deep green and cream.

By 1905 the estimates had climbed to £59,144 and the Committee were considering seeking additional borrowing powers, but thought it best to defer until it was known what sum would be required. As the Chairman of the Baths and Wash-houses Committee, William Thomas Rothwell, stated in his letter of 26 July 1905,

> With regard to the total probable expenditure of £59,144, the Committee beg to inform the Council that their desire throughout has been to have these Victoria Baths properly adapted in every detail for the purpose they have to serve. This has increased the first cost but the baths are so constructed that it is anticipated that the cost of maintenance will be materially reduced.[15]

Just over a year later, on Friday, 7 September 1906, Victoria Baths were opened by the Lord Mayor who described the Baths as 'a Water Palace of which every citizen of Manchester is proud'.

Notes
1 C. Francis, *Welfare of the Needy* (1971), p. 27.
2 James Phillips Kay MD, *The Moral & Physical Conditions of the Working Classes* (1832), pp. 30-1.
3 G. F. Pardon, *The Manchester Conductor* (1857), pp. 40-1.
4 Manchester Central Library, Historical Tracts H837.
5 Manchester Central Library, News Cuttings Box 115.
6 *How Manchester is Managed* (1936), p. 106.
7 Ibid., (1926), pp. 172-3.
8 Council Minutes, (1904-5), vol. 3, p. 487.
9 Ibid., p. 489.
10 Ibid., p. 490.
11 Ibid., p. 488.
12 Ibid., p. 489.
13 Ibid., p. 495.
14 Ibid., p. 504.
15 Ibid., p. 496

CHAPTER 2

INSIDE THE BATHS

Whatever '… slings and arrows of outrageous fortune'[1] may have attended the planning and building of Victoria Baths, there is no doubt that the richness of the end result has made a profound and long-lasting impression on the hearts and minds of all who have memories of using these baths.

It is a breathtaking experience on entering this extraordinary building by the First Class Males door to see the wonders of architectural excellence which await us within. Before the artistic wrought-iron work of the turnstile is a list of the Councillors who battled over the ten years or so of planning and building this 'Water Palace'. This commemorative plaque recording the opening of Victoria Baths by the Lord Mayor, Herbert Thewliss, J.P., on 7 September 1906 is signed by George Wragge of Salford and fittingly framed by a beautiful glass mosaic in floral Art Nouveau style. This is in turn surrounded by a deep green outer frame of large ornate faience.

Then on through the rich polish of baywood, pitchpine and stained glass which make up the inner doors. A celebration in deep green and cream tiling bursts upon our vision. We stop and stare at the magnificent staircase with its sturdy ceramic balustrades supporting the wide handrail, all in the prevailing deep green glaze. This, and the matching wall-tiling, contrasts beautifully with the cream tiling above. As we gaze our fill, we realise we are standing on yet another wonder of the entrance hall, the mosaic flooring with its design of leaping fish and fat little dolphins frolicking among the sea flora on waves leading to the First Class Males pool hall.

The First Class entrance hall is by far the most ornate, with floor-to-ceiling tiles, mosaic floors and an impressive ceramic balustrade on the staircase.

The First Class Males/Gala Pool in 1906. It still looks very similar in 2004.

To the left of the entrance hall are double doors leading to the area which used to house the First Class Males wash baths. When the need for wash baths declined, the baths were removed and replaced by changing facilities to suit the large classes of school children who used to change here.

The First Class Males/Gala Pool is the largest of the three pools, 75 feet by 40 feet, compared to the other two pools measuring 75 feet by 35 feet and 75 feet by 30 feet. Changing cubicles constructed in glazed brick and cast-iron with solid wooden doors line both sides of the pool. At the far end, above the central arch, is the foundation stone dated 1903. Looking up we see along two sides and one end, the railings of the viewing gallery. Again, no expense was spared to make this worthy of the showpiece Victoria swimming baths. The main approach to the gallery is from the entrance hall by that splendid ceramic staircase, through a vestibule of pitchpine with stained glass windows. Two extra staircases were provided, one at the end of each side gallery. This gallery is suspended from steel stanchions built in the main walls. The floors are tongued-and-grooved pitchpine boards. The gallery front has beautiful ornamental wrought-iron railings with polished baywood handrails. The walls around the gallery are of glazed brick below, with buff bricks above, picked out in red. There are patent automatic shut-up seats for 236 persons and standing room for 110 persons.[2] This provided seating in two tiers with good viewing facilities for parents who came to watch their sons and daughters taking part in school and club galas. Here too enthusiastic supporters cheered on their teams in the county championships and diving events.

Now, sadly, the pool is empty of water, the balcony empty of spectators but standing in this evocative pool hall and listening carefully, we can almost hear the echoes and shouts of encouragement and young voices' laughter as yet another gala comes to a successful climax and competitors and spectators make their way to the cubicles and the refreshment area. Many thousands of people have swum here over the years.

Nellie Ryder with the Wilson Challenge Shield which she won in 1917.

Helen 'Nellie' Ryder was born in 1904 and became a pupil at Ducie Avenue Central School and a member of the Victoria Swimming Club. Her sister Marion was also a keen swimmer and member of the club. She won the Wilson Challenge Shield in 1917, a trophy which Zilpha Grant would later win in 1930. Helen married Frederick McGrath in 1928 and brought up eleven children. She continued swimming until the age of ninety.[3]

Erica Bury was born in 1907 and grew up in Levenshulme. She joined the Victoria Swimming Club and trained hard until she earned a place on the ladies swimming team. When she started work for the Liverpool London and Globe Insurance Company, she represented her firm at the Manchester Annual Insurance Swimming Gala, winning five first prizes. In due course she became Erica Chesworth after meeting and marrying Thomas Chesworth. They had three children who all learnt to swim at an early age. When her eldest children joined the South Manchester Swimming Club, Erica became a coach at the club. Training was every Monday evening with galas held on Friday evenings. Erica was eventually made a life member of the club in the 1950s in appreciation of her dedication and services to the club. Her daughter writes:

> An annual gala was held for the swimming club every September and every member could take part who wished to do so. There were events for every type of swimmer from the novices to the hopeful Olympic swimmers. Many of the

races had a silver trophy for the winner to hold for one year, along with a prize for the first three in each race.

Erica Chesworth lived to the age of 95 and was swimming until she was 90.[4]

Most Manchester schools used to hold their annual swimming gala at Victoria Baths. The Burnage High School Magazine for December 1936 described the school's Annual Gala as follows:

> *October 6 –* The second Annual Swimming Gala was held at the Victoria Baths, High Street, at 7pm. There was a large crowd of parents and jubilant, vivacious schoolboys, who listened eagerly as the announcer read out the names of the competitors and then said "Go". Each competitor, determined to win glory for his House, if possible, ploughed his way through the water, or plunged with utmost neatness and skill. Nothing can be so glorious, so memorable, as a gala. In the cheering, the merry chaffing and quick repartee, in the applause for a splendid win, and in the keen, thorough rivalry, exempt from malice, the true spirit of the School reveals itself. Both spectators and competitors shared in the enthusiasm which was manifest throughout. To no small extent was the success of the evening dependent on the splendid organisation and due to the kindness of the following swimmers, whom we cordially thank for their exhibitions:

Miss S. Lowry (Channel Swimmer, 1933)
Mr. S. Vernon (Northern Counties' and Lancashire Junior Free Style Champion)
Mr. P. Rastall (Northern Counties' and Lancashire Free Style
Champion, 1932-3)
Mr. C. Peck (exhibition of plain and trick swimming)

Changing cubicles in the First Class Males pool.

CHAPTER 2

The First Class Males Pool 2003.

Erica Bury (left), having been awarded the Bronze Medallion, *c.* 1923.

Northern Counties' Ladies Squadron Champions, 1933-4-5
Pupils trained by Mr. J. Laverty and Miss N. Laverty
Master R. Gannon (South Manchester S/c)
We also thank J. Tonks, Esq., N.C.A.S.A., for rendering such willing and efficient service as official starter.

The 'pupils trained by Miss N. Laverty' in the 1930s were a group of girls who became known as the 'Water Babies'. They performed what we would now call synchronised swimming, not as a competitive activity, but for performance at events such as the gala described above. Mrs Irene Stanley, as a child, was a good friend of Doreen Laverty, Miss Laverty's niece. The two girls spent many happy hours at Victoria Baths under the supervision of 'Auntie Nellie'.[5]

Many people remember supporting their friends and classmates prepare for the Annual Inter-schools Swimming Gala. Alan Williams writes:

Boys competing in the inter-towns gala, 1973 (photo David Montford).

My memory of Victoria Baths is that it was a little special to go there. I was a schoolboy at Princess Road Junior School and we normally went to Broadfield Baths. Occasionally we would go to Victoria Baths and we had a double-decker bus to take us. I imagine it was to get our swimming team ready for the inter-school Swimming Gala. This I remember very well as we [the spectators] were seated upstairs overlooking the pool. When each race started, the noise from excited schoolchildren was deafening.[6]

The beautiful stained glass windows above the foundation stone and the main spectator entrance are still overlooking the scene where so much has happened over the past century. So many vivid memories live on in the hearts and minds of all who are a part of the living history of this most elaborate and spectacular bathhouse. They tell their stories on their visits to our Open Days, some going back to the fifties, forties, thirties and in a few cases even to the 1920s, as if it were only yesterday.

Erica Bury and four other members of the Victoria Swimming Club *c.*1927.

One lady recalled being filmed because she could swim a length of backstroke with a cup of water balanced on her forehead.[7] The swimming teachers are fondly remembered. The ladies often speak of Nellie Laverty. Her training sessions were strict and thorough but very much enjoyed and the rewards came when the girls picked up their medals and prizes at local and county championships.[8] Another lady who remembers Miss Nellie Laverty started her swimming career early at the tender age of five. She tells of her parents paying a guinea (£1 1s. 0d) for 10 lessons. When she was seven she was entered in the swimming gala to do 25 yards breaststroke. She came in last to great cheers and was given her prize, a huge box of chocolates![9] The water polo matches were very popular, especially with the girls. One of our lady visitors said that they looked on the water polo players as gods.[10]

Our gentlemen visitors too have their memories and, inspired by seeing the lovely setting of their youthful endeavours still intact, they respond by telling their stories and bringing the past of Victoria Baths back to life. One man spoke of the ritual of washing in the hot water trough before being allowed into the pool. He said it was very difficult to wash properly while wearing a swimming costume because the soap dissolved too quickly![11] Another recalled winning a wallet in the Gala competition. He also spoke of boys swimming naked in the 1940s in the Males Second Class pool. He said he and his pals tried their best to find out if the girl swimmers did the same![12] One Manchester resident recalls spending his Saturday mornings in the war years diving in the deep end of Victoria Baths for sixpences thrown in by American GIs sitting in the balcony.[13]

Our visitors cannot understand why the baths were ever closed and express their support for our endeavours and their hopes that

A programme for a Swimming Club trip, to Cheltenham, Bristol and Weston-super-Mare in July/August 1949.

Girls receiving prizes at the 1973 Inter-towns gala (photo David Montford).

this magnificent example of Edwardian architecture will be saved for the benefit of future generations of Mancunians and visitors to our lovely city.

There are many more memories, so many that they deserve a book to themselves but I cannot leave out just one more going back to the very early days when the sexes were strictly divided. In 1914, mixed bathing had been introduced on a trial basis 'with great caution' at Withington Baths. This proved to be a huge success.[14] Always ready to accept new ideas, Victoria Baths followed and in 1922 allowed mixed bathing each Tuesday from 2pm. Charges were 6d for adults and 3d for juniors.[15] One of our ladies, who went on to become a famous swimmer, started her career at Victoria Baths in 1919 before mixed

Above: The Males Second Class Pool, showing troughs for pre-washing, wash bath cubicles on the balcony and swimming instruction in progress c.1928.
Opposite: The Males Second Class Pool being boarded over to convert it to a Sports Hall c.1986.

bathing was allowed. She remembers getting changed for a gala in the cubicles of the Females Pool, then being led in line with the other girls competing to their position in the Gala Pool. As they walked through their lady instructor told them to 'turn your heads the other way, girls'. The Males Pool cubicles had no curtains and the men and boys were in various states of undress![16]

Apart from its use for galas, the First Class Males Pool was designed for use by males who had to pay extra for the privilege of using water from the well first, before it was returned to the two storage tanks at the rear of the pool halls to be used in the Second Class Males and the Females Pools. At least this is the story which has been passed down the years. Certainly the First Class swimmers had the benefit of a much more ornate entrance hall, more spacious changing facilities and a larger pool.

Although the water in all three pools was so much improved by the 1930s, people were still prepared to pay the extra coppers for the luxury of swimming in the First Class Pool. An added attraction was chute and diving platforms. These used to be at the far end just in front of the arches into the shower area. However, they were removed later when it was deemed unsafe to dive into six feet of water.

We have spent quite some time describing the Males First Class or Gala Pool hall, but the other two pools were also an essential part of the Baths and are fondly remembered by many of our visitors. Today the Second Class Males pool hall looks light and airy and the roof is in relatively good condition. This is because in the 1980s the Council renovated the pool hall making it into an indoor Sports Hall. The changing cubicles were taken out and the pool was covered over and marked out for five-a-side football, badminton, netball and basketball. The original bathtubs, which lined the balcony, were taken out and the floor made good. The balcony was then used for table tennis, running and as a practice area for the Manchester tug o' war teams.[18]

CHAPTER 2

Water treatment through the years

At the turn of the twentieth century when Victoria Baths was built, swimming pools or 'plunges' were operated on the 'fill and empty' principle, so the water got cloudier as the week went on.

At Victoria Baths the pools were emptied twice a week. The tiles on the sides and bottom were scrubbed clean and the pool refilled with the water stored in the huge tanks above the boiler houses at the back of the building.

In the Female Pool, Mondays and Thursdays were 'clean days' when the pool was refilled. On those days the admission charge in 1922 was 6d, the first class cost. After three days of use the water would become decidedly cloudy and somewhat smelly, so Wednesdays and Saturdays were 'dirty days' when women and girls could swim for 4d, the lower second class charge.

Things had changed by the 1930s. In the 1930 City Council report *How Manchester is Managed* there are details of swimming provision and a description of 'How the Water is kept clean':

There was a time when the cleanliness of the water in swimming baths depended mainly on the number of times the baths were emptied and refilled. Now, however, each baths is fitted with ingenious filtering and aerating plant, with pumps worked mostly by electric motors. By its means the water is always fresh and inviting. ... A further development is that the Victoria and Chorlton Baths have all been equipped with a chlorinating plant, and during the coming winter eight other establishments are to be similarly improved.[17]

Going back in time, there used to be 23 wash baths in the gallery of the Males Second Class pool in cubicles of varnished pitchpine and this amenity was very much appreciated. Many of our gentlemen visitors speak of enjoying a weekly 'proper bath' here. There were also footbaths or troughs on the poolside in each pool hall where swimmers had to have a wash before entering the swimming pool. These were filled with warm water and soap provided. Many people remember these troughs or 'tubs'. Although provided for washing, they were used by children for warming up because the water in them was considerably warmer than the pool water. 'We stayed in the plunge until we were frozen then proceeded to the tubs, squeezed in so tightly so that we sat with our bottoms in the spreadeagled legs of the swimmers behind us until another person could not get in.'[19]

plan had been to send the towels and other linen from Victoria Baths to Mayfield Wash-house. When this proved to be impossible, the decision was taken to provide an establishment wash-house at Victoria Baths. So, plans were amended, extra money was found, and Victoria Wash-house was built.

But that is not the end of the story. Having got their wash-house, built primarily as an establishment laundry, its role throughout the coming years was extended to allow the public to use its facilities whenever the need arose. This, according to many people, happened quite often, sometimes recorded in official papers, sometimes not. So Victoria Wash-house lives on in the memory of many of our visitors, as the place to which their weekly wash was trundled in little carts or prams. The ladies were so grateful to escape the drudgery of washing day in the home with its discomfort and danger to health. By contrast, the

Free Baths for the Unemployed

The special facilities given to the unemployed of the city to use the second-class baths – both wash and swimming – free of charge between the hours of 9 a.m. and 12 noon during the summer and between 9 a.m. and 4 p.m. in winter were taken advantage of by 16,609 persons as compared with 12,576 in 1928-9 and 10,315 in 1926-7. The concession was first made in 1922-3, and then 8,456 tickets were issued. In each case a personal application must be made to the General Superintendent.

How Manchester is Managed, 1930, p. 41.

weekly visit to the wash-house became almost a social occasion, where one could meet up with friends and enjoy a good old gossip.

In the wash-house the average family wash was placed in the rotary washing machines, the necessary operation of working the valves for the water, steam etc., for soaking, boiling and rinsing being done by the attendant. After washing, the clothes were put into a hydro-extractor, which speedily removed most of the moisture; the clothes were then placed in the drying chamber, and so on to the ironing room for completion in about two hours.[10]

Mrs May Flanaghan, née Tatton, now 97, started work as the attendant at Victoria Wash-house in 1919 when she was just 14. She also had office work to do and, as a junior employee, some cleaning jobs. The ironing tables had to be scrubbed, also the steps to the baths and wash-house. May remembers Nellie Laverty, who was in charge of the ladies' pool, and Miss Redfearn who she says was also a good instructress.

She also tells of Mr Teasdale, the Baths Superintendent: 'He watched staff and customers like a hawk'. He was very strict but May got on well with him. She was a cycling enthusiast and he always enquired about her weekend activities.

It was like a madhouse, she says, when the kids came to swim, clamouring at the ticket office for their ha'penny tickets. Some would dive off the balcony to avoid having to pay.

The wash-house must have been open to the public when May first worked there as she speaks of the ladies bringing their own soap to keep down the expense. It cost 3d per wash. There was no limit to the amount of washing. 'Mounds of it', said May.

One of the perks of her job was that sometimes she would be given a pawn ticket by one or other of her customers. 'Here y'are mate, I can't afford to redeem my bundle', she would be told. May would then exchange the ticket for a bundle of filthy linen, which she would give several washes, until the tablecloths, sheets and other linen came out sparkling white. She has a bedding chest full of good-quality linen of which she is very proud, all given her in this fashion, so her friend and neighbour tells me.[11] May has fond memories of the long, airy room with the electrically powered rotary washing machines, mangles and hydros.

Under the system of advance booking there was no waiting at the wash-house. People would simply apply at the ticket office and book a machine at an hour most suitable to themselves.[12] So there was no

For many years the water at Victoria Baths was heated by coal-fired boilers made by Galloways.

trouble about whose turn it was to use the washing machines. It was when it came to putting the washing into the hydros occasionally arguments and even fights would break out.

But May, by all accounts, ruled her wash-house with a rod of iron and quickly restored order.[13] Then the washing was hung on the drying racks and hot air was blown in from the furnaces. When dry it was taken to the ironing room for completion. The irons were the ordinary flat irons which had to be heated on ironing stoves. May had to scrub the three long tables on which the ironing was done. Some of the women took in washing - that is they did other people's washing and ironing to earn a little money to help feed the family.

The ironing stoves and the furnaces were fuelled by coke. It was a field day for the children of the neighbourhood when the coke was delivered, they would retrieve any that was spilt and sometimes helped to spill more, so they could have a fire on at home.

They were long hard days when May first worked at Victoria Baths, from 7.30 in the morning until 8 o'clock in the evening, but she was not afraid of hard work and proved it by working for 43 years at the job she loved. May was such a capable person that in times of need she would be asked to help out at other wash-houses.

One of her vivid memories is of doing a few early Monday morning stints at Ancoats Wash-house.

CHAPTER 4

The wash-house at Victoria Baths was built as an establishment laundry.

She tells of the prostitutes coming in early to wash their one set of good clothes. They would have a bath and then sit around naked waiting for their clothes to dry. The ladies got on well with May. They told her that when they got home they would change into their weekday clothes and put the ones they had just laundered on to hangers to be ready for their next weekend. Then it was back to Victoria Baths for the rest of the long day for May, but she always coped.

There were improvements as time went by; she had extra help and shorter working hours. Electric irons replaced the old flat irons, the washing machines and hydro extractors were kept in good working order and eventually replaced by more efficient modern machines.

May made many friends over her long career, and, like most people who worked at Victoria Baths, speaks of the 'family' atmosphere prevailing there.

May had married Mr Flanaghan and their son, Peter, was born shortly before the Second World War,

Exhibition of Manchester City Council, Baths & Wash-houses Department, 1932.

so when her husband went into the army, May left Manchester with Peter to stay with her sister for a short while. Her time away may have coincided with the closure of Victoria Baths. Mr Teasdale announced at an emergency meeting that the Baths would be closing until further notice, and all Club activities would be suspended indefinitely.[14]

The Baths did not stay closed for long. By November 1939 May was back in her wash-house, the three pools had been re-opened, and although Club fixtures had been cancelled, whist drives were being held in the Coffee Room in the basement and plans to hold a dance evening were being discussed.[15]

So it was 'Business as Usual' at High Street Baths, although the increasing number of members of H.M. Forces in uniform taking advantage of bathing facilities at the special rate of 1d. reminded one that there was a war on. Also, as part of the Air Raid Precautions Scheme, the Baths Department was made responsible for the decontamination of clothing, and staff were trained in this work to be carried out in the wash-houses should the necessity arise.[16]

Fortunately the anticipated enemy gas attacks did not materialise, but in December 1940 came the savage Christmas attacks on the centre of Manchester. For two nights, on 22 and 23 December, hundreds of enemy planes dropped incendiaries, bombs and land mines on the almost defenceless civilians, causing many deaths and injuries and reducing their houses, offices and shops to rubble. Victoria Baths was undamaged, but the Leaf Street and Mayfield Baths and Wash-houses were so severely damaged that it proved impossible to re-open them.[17] This put pressure on other wash-houses and May was busier than ever. As such a cheerful and capable person, she would be doing her bit to boost the morale of the hard-working ladies using the laundry facilities and moaning about food shortages and rationing.

But it was not all doom and gloom. As we will see in another chapter, the Dance Nights at Victoria became a much-loved feature of the war years. For most of the post-war decade, it seems that the wash-house at Victoria Baths reverted to being an establishment laundry.

May did not retire until 1962, so she was still running her wash-house when it was next re-opened to the public in 1960.

Neil Bonner, Treasurer of the Friends of Victoria Baths, trustee of the Victoria Baths Trust, and regular tour guide on Open Days, has a vivid memory of his mother taking the weekly wash to Victoria Baths. This was because their usual wash-house at South Street, across Stockport Road, had been closed for maintenance work. Neil is sad when he sees the empty wash-house now when he recalls his mum telling him some of the tales of using the dryer and the ironer.

Neil's family used to live in a newsagent's shop on Stockport Road and his mother was introduced to South Street Wash-house by their shop assistant Mary Seaton who knew that Mrs Bonner had to wash for five children and was very busy during the day. They used to stand their wash baskets in large prams and go for the first wash at 7am so they could be back to see the children off to school and allow Neil's father to go to bed after working nights. Neil wouldn't assist his mother with the weekly wash – although girls were allowed to go into the wash-house, boys were strictly forbidden. He would sometimes see his mum as he walked to Plymouth Grove School if she was late home owing to someone beating her to the quicker machines or dryers.

> **Manchester City Council were clearly proud of their wash-houses as the following extract shows:**
>
> Excellent though the swimming baths may be, it is in the provision of public washhouses that the Baths and Washhouses Committee finds most satisfaction. Amongst all the civic services there is probably nothing to which the housewife could give greater praise than to the public washhouse. By taking her washing there she not only saves time and money, but she experiences the joys mentioned in the advertisements - i.e., she watches the machines do the work, and at the same time preserves her schoolgirl complexion.
>
> Centenary Celebration of Manchester's Incorporation, 1938, *Official Handbook to the Exhibition of Civic Services*, Baths and Washhouses Section, p. 83.

Chapter 4

Notes

1 *How Manchester is Managed* (1936), p. 41

2 Mr K. Allen, memory sheet, 11-12 September 1999.

3 George Robert Kinder, letter, 31 May 2002.

4 Nancy Dudley, letter, 24 November 1999.

5 Mrs M. Mitchell, memory sheet, 11-12 September 1999.

6 June Zentek, née Roberts, e-mail, 8 May 2001.

7 *Manchester Evening News*, 27 August 1904.

8 Plan by A. Davies, Manchester Corporation's Surveyor, July 1901.

9 Plan by Henry Price, City Architect, 2 October 1902.

10 Centenary Booklet of Manchester Baths & Wash-houses, pp. 6, 7.

11 Mrs Renée Diaz, phone call, 13 Sepember 2002.

12 As note 10, p. 7.

13 Mrs Renée Diaz, phone call, 6 November 2002.

14 South Manchester Swimming Club, Minute Book, Emergency Meeting, 1 September 1939.

15 South Manchester Swimming Club, Minute Book, 9 November 1939.

16. Manchester City Council Report on Baths & Washhouses (1940-1), p. 5.

17 Ibid., p. 3.

CHAPTER 5

TURKISH BATHS & AERATONE

The slipper baths, or wash baths, were not the only much appreciated wash facility at Victoria. The Turkish Baths too were very popular, and are now sadly missed by their devotees. One writes as follows:

> I was interested to read your website, not least because the trip from Manchester to Harrogate for my weekly Turkish Bath is ruinously expensive! When are you expecting to re-open? I can just remember coming to the baths as a small child, I think the excitement left an indelible mark on me. I still love Victoria Baths, and am an evangelical Turkish Bath fan. Many of my friends whom I see at my local leisure centre sauna and in Harrogate are looking forward with barely contained excitement to being able to have a proper Turkish Bath in Manchester again. There's a great wave of support for you amongst everyone I know, and we wish you all speed and best wishes.[1]

The Tepidarium and Russian Bath in the Turkish Baths suite, 1906.

So what is there about these Turkish Baths? Many people feel they are most beneficial and believe they can act as a deterrent to rheumatic ailments, and a cure for sprains and strains.

There are different ways of using Turkish Baths; some people prefer to go from cool to hot, and others prefer the opposite direction. A 1939 description states:

> In the Turkish Baths, the bathers are subjected to a gradually increasing temperature until a copious perspiration has broken out. After a time they pass to rooms of decreasing temperature until they reach the shampooing room, where they are massaged and shampooed, then doused with warm, tepid and cold water, rubbed down, wrapped in a warm towel and

The sumptuous Rest Room of the Turkish Baths suite, 1906.

Spotless & Warm

Elizabeth Grayson, born in Salford and now living in London, wrote enthusing on her memories of going to the High Street Baths.

The Baths were always spotlessly clean, warm and comfortable. I remember going to the Turkish Baths in 1955, a particularly hot summer (better than 2003). The cost was 5/- for say two and a half hours. On arrival we were each allotted a cotton "shift" and a deck chair. We could move at will from warm to hot room to hotter room with, at the end, a needle sharp circular shower. There was no jacuzzi (hadn't been invented then) but we were 'flogged' at the end of the session with bunches of twigs, by a very large but kindly lady. Then we were invited to lie on the leather couches and given afternoon tea – buttered muffins, I think, and tea. It was all very enjoyable, much nicer than saunas (I always call these poor man's Turkish Baths).[10]

allowed to rest until the body has resumed its normal temperature. The effect of the bath is the removal of a large amount of waste matter and poisons from the body, which leaves the bather feeling in the best of health and mentally alert.[2]

At Victoria Baths, the exuberant setting of the upper Turkish Rest Room reflects the aura of indulgent luxury of this facility. As the bathers relax, they enjoy the beauty of the wonderful stained glass windows, the daylight flowing down from the glass-panelled ceiling, the curtained cubicles, the marvellous green patterned wall tiling and the carpeted floor. There is even an example of Edwardian double-glazing. The stained glass windows between the Laconicum and the Rest Room are so built to conserve the heat in the hottest room of the Turkish Bath suite. There was also a lower Rest Room, with beds for relaxation, reached by a fine balustraded stairway from the upper Rest Room.

Presiding triumphantly over all this luxury is the large, very colourful 'Angel of Purity' window. The statuesque angel figure is balancing on a lily pond and holding white lilies. The whole vibrant Art Nouveau scene gives the impression of air, light, water, warmth and all the good things in life, just to emphasise the feelings of well-being experienced after enjoying the Turkish Bath. And the cost for all this luxury? From 1922 to 1947 it was 2s. 6d, rising to 7s. 6d in 1964. The price rose steadily and in the years before closure people were paying £3.00. But there was no decline in numbers of people using the Turkish Baths; if anything they became more popular and

The 'Angel of Purity' still presides over the Turkish Baths Rest Room.

HOT AIR BATHS

Many types of hot air bath have been used in Europe and the area surrounding the Mediterranean during the past millennium. Here are some of the most popular:

Roman baths. The Romans did not invent the hot air bath but their invention of the hypocaust (underfloor heating system) enabled them to perfect it. At its simplest, the Roman bath consisted of a number of interconnected rooms heated by hot air passing under the floors of each room in turn. The room nearest to the furnace (the *laconicum*) was the hottest. Then came the ordinary hot room (the *caldarium*) and, furthest from the furnace, the coolest of the hot rooms (the *tepidarium*). Because the heated air was *underneath* the floor, the hot air in the rooms was dry – with a complete absence of steam. Bathers spent time in each room in turn before finishing with a dip in an adjacent cold plunge pool and a resting period in a cooling room (the *frigidarium*). Roman *thermae* often also included separate steam baths, gymnasia, swimming pools and libraries, but these were all additional to the Roman bath itself.

The Islamic *hammam* developed from the hot air baths in the Eastern Roman Empire. Unlike the Romans, Muslims believe that the body should remain covered during the bathing process. They therefore omitted the adjacent plunge pool, adding decorative fountains and washing facilities round the walls of the main hot room. The mixture of the hot air with the washing water makes the air in the *hammam* very humid, and frequently misty or even steamy. Like the Roman baths, *hammams* often have additional steam baths where washing also takes place.

The vapour, steam, medicated, or Russian bath. In these baths the bather sits in a room into which steam is fed and the bather starts to perspire very quickly. Today these baths have become popular as they can be prefabricated and are cheap to run. They are often mistakenly called Turkish baths.

The Victorian Turkish bath. This is actually a Roman bath in appearance and effect, though some are heated by blowing hot dry air through the rooms themselves, instead of passing it under the floors. Under the influence of David Urquhart (1805-77), the first such bath opened near Cork in 1856, and the first in England opened the following year in Manchester. Because Urquhart had discovered the hot air bath in Turkey, it became known as the Turkish bath – or later, because the air was dry, the Improved Turkish Bath. When these baths crossed the channel to Europe they were often known as Irish-Roman baths.

Our so-called Turkish bath at the Victoria Baths is actually a Roman bath because the hot air was absolutely dry and the bather spent time in a series of increasingly hot rooms. Only a handful of such baths remain in the British Isles today.

The sauna. In a sauna the air is heated by a stove (these days usually electric) in the hot room itself. The heating elements are covered by stones which retain the heat. Bathers can adjust the humidity (or dampness) of the hot air by splashing water onto the stones. This creates a sort of halfway house between the Russian steam bath and the Victorian Turkish bath.

Malcolm Shifrin, Victorian Turkish Bath Project, www.victorianturkishbath.org

were well-used right up to the time the Baths closed in 1993.

The Turkish Baths, as well as providing rest and relaxation, have been a popular meeting place for business people over the years. It seems that many a deal has been struck, or a new business venture planned by customers lying naked or semi-naked in the hot rooms, or whilst cooling off in the opulent Rest Room.

One of our visitors has commented:

> For a forty-year period I frequented the Baths. The Turkish Baths were very popular, a huge contingent of Mancunians used it. Many athletes came, also boxers, wrestlers and Manchester City and Manchester United footballers. There was an enormous atmosphere of camaraderie.[3]

Another gentleman writes: 'I came to the Turkish Baths from 1986 to 1992. I remember all nationalities going down there on Friday afternoons, Sikhs, English, West Indians, Polish, all together. A welcome community spirit'.[4]

Paul Mason obviously loved the Turkish Baths and explained that he attended four times a week from 1972 until closure in 1993. In a phone call he enthused over the facilities of the Rest Room, which in his time had had T.V. installed. An attendant would bring drinks and the bathers relaxed in a Gentleman's Club atmosphere. Some brought their lunch or a snack and there was always a rich flow of friendly conversation between people of all nationalities.[5]

The ladies, too, enjoyed the Turkish Baths. Their days were Monday and Thursday, which seems a bit unfair as the men had the other four days. Certainly Ladies' Days were reported to be busy. One lady writes:

> I came on Thursday evenings before the baths closed, I think that was the ladies' evening. We used the Turkish

Baths and Russian Baths. I was quite overwhelmed by the interior décor, and amazed at the turnstile and the wonderful staircase. I went with a group of friends. We all enjoyed the happy relaxing atmosphere. I was very upset when I heard the baths were to be closed. I very much miss my weekly sessions of the Turkish Baths in such beautiful surroundings.[6]

Another lady enthuses:

In the Turkish Bath there was a feeling of timelessness. I thought, this could be any age or time. In the steam and the quiet, snippets of conversation and laughter. I was new to the city, and here I was with Asian women, Afro-Caribbean women, using special scrubs and oils, coconut smells. Asian women, usually covered, laughed and gossiped. As an artist I wanted to capture this experience, but never had the courage to pull out a sketch book. This place should remain the private domain of trust between these women.[7]

Above and right: Stained glass in the Turkish Baths Rest Room.

A group of friends met up regularly on Thursday mornings to go for their weekly sessions in the luxury of Victoria Turkish Baths. It was their time for relaxation and getting away from it all. Margery Hoey says: 'I came to the Turkish Baths every week and missed it very much when it closed. My two friends, Mrs Bradbury and Joyce Lomas came with me. It was always busy on Ladies' Days.'[8] Mrs Bradbury tells of the enjoyable Thursday morning sessions. She too remembers how busy the Turkish Baths were and how difficult it was to book places for more friends to come. She says it was lovely to relax amid the beauty of the upper Rest Room where they could enjoy a drink or a snack if they wished. She says it was a great shame when the Turkish Baths closed and hopes they

will soon be open again.[9]

The people who worked at the Turkish Baths Suite in the 1960s are often mentioned by our visitors on Open Days. The ladies remember Jessie, who looked after the Turkish Baths on Ladies' Days. Mary McDonough, who made snacks and drinks for the bathers is fondly remembered by both men and ladies. Her daughter writes,

> Our Mum used to make tea and snacks, beans, cheese, egg on toast for the Turkish and Aeratone bathers. I went to St Joseph's School, after school I would go to Victoria Baths to help Mum. When it was Ladies' Day we could go into the Rest Room to collect towels, cups, plates and trays, but on the Men's Days we had to collect things from a shelf after knocking on the door. I can remember the heat in the Turkish Baths Suite, even after it had closed for the day. I saw Matt Busby's wife. Many wrestlers came, but I can't remember their names. One unforgettable Turkish Bath devotee was Tommy Cooper.[11]

The Aeratone

Another very popular facility at Victoria Baths was the Aeratone or, to give it its full title, the Aeratone Therapeutic Bath. It was the forerunner of the Jacuzzi and was invented by a Scotsman, Professor William Oliver, who came down to Manchester to supervise personally the installation of the

Stained glass in the Turkish Baths Rest Room.

Aeratone at Victoria Baths in 1952.[12]

A newspaper article of the time states: 'Valuable in the treatment of rheumatic diseases, the aeratone therapeutic bath is the first of its kind in England and will be open to the public on 3 July 1952, at Victoria Baths, High Street, Manchester.' The accompanying picture shows Councillor William Swan

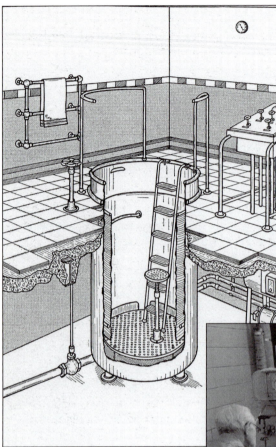

enjoying the new 'bubble bath'.[13] It quickly became so popular that there was always a waiting list of people wanting to book their half-hour session.

One of the visitors tells us: 'I only had two goes in the Aeratone because it was so difficult to book. If Fred had it at 4.00 on Friday, he'd book it again for the same time the following week. It was like waiting for dead men's shoes!'[14]

Jackie Kerr describes it very graphically: 'You climbed up and into the Aeratone Bath. It was more intense than the modern jacuzzi, with "needles" of water rather than jets. Very much more like a massage.'[15]

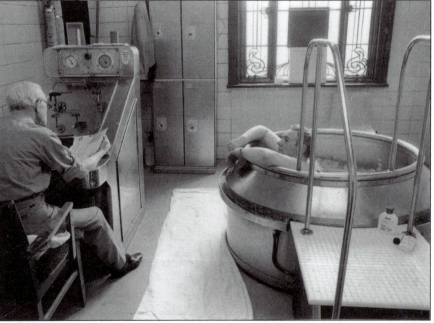

Top: The Aeratone Therapeutic Bath – a 'powerful hydraulic machine for applying a controlled vibrating massage to all parts of the immersed body simultaneously' (Publicity brochure, c.1950).
Bottom: The Aeratone at Victoria Baths in use in 1986 (photo: David Montford).

CHAPTER 5

An even more graphic description of an Aeratone experience is recalled in a personal memoir by Ian McRae. He writes: 'For a number of years before the closure of Victoria Baths I visited the baths once or twice a week during my lunch break from work in the adjacent Norweb building. Sometime I swam, other times I used the Aeratone.

The Aeratone was an impressive installation, a stainless steel 'conning tower' standing a couple of feet above the floor, with access ladder to facilitate ascent of the rim and descent into the deep stainless steel tub with room for one. A stainless steel high tech control panel (temperature, agitation rate etc.) was adjacent and under the control of a trained member of staff who prepared the settings in advance for each client, registered in advance for an exclusive session of 30 minutes. In the discrete privacy of the Aeratone room complete undress was possible with modesty and was normal. During this period of my ablutionary development, I had been persuaded, by a relative, of the pleasurable benefit of using in my domestic bath water, a green substance known commercially as Badedas. The odour was certainly attractive and refreshing and it occurred to me that a small quantity of this substance could enhance the pleasure of aeratone bathing and I determined to try the experience.

I attended the Aeratone Suite at an appointed time equipped with a small bottle of the green substance in addition to my towel and other accessories. The attendant was fully prepared for me with temperature and flow pressure accurately adjusted and stabilised. We acknowledged each other in the casual manner which was our custom and he then assured me that all was ready and, as he had other work to deal with, if I was happy to be left for a few minutes. Of course I was happy!

Prepared to bathe in my usual state of undress, I measured a small capful of the Badedas and emptied this into the gently foaming hot water …

The foaming was miraculously, astonishingly, ALARMINGLY (in sequence much more speedy than the time to read!) from gentle to explosive, the 'conning tower' was suddenly full, then overflowing! In less time than it takes to imagine the sequence of events, the whole room was six inches – then nine inches – then a foot deep in perfumed bubbles.

I consider that I am normally more than usually capable of dealing with the unexpected. I can now confirm that enterprise in the seeking of assistance to deal with the unexpected is much reduced by nudity. Fortunately, while I was still pondering on my options, the Aeratone operative returned and managed to switch off the pump before I had become submerged, possibly forever, in Badedas foam.

I cannot remember the subsequent reaction of the operative – I understand that the human brain has a fail-safe mechanism which prevents the permanent registration of alarm above a certain critical level. I do, however, recall that during my period of uncertain pondering, I became aware at first hand of the difficulties of decision-making experienced by Stan Laurel.

CHAPTER 5

Notes

1 Andrew Teather, e-mail, 7 October 2002.

2 *How Manchester Managed* (1939), p. 163.

3 Mr L. Dartington, memory sheet, 9 September 2001.

4 Mr Rich Tundi, memory sheet, 12 September 1999.

5 Paul Mason, memory sheet, 12 March 2000 and phone call 10 April 2003.

6 Alison Thompson, memory sheet, 12 September 1999.

7 Alison Kershaw, memory sheet, 12 March 2000.

8 Margery Hoey, memory sheet, 12 September 1999.

9 Mrs Bradbury, telephone call, 16 April 2003.

10 Elizabeth Grayson, letter, 20 January 2004.

11 Pat McDonough, memory sheet, 12 March 2000.

12 Mrs Oliver, telephone call, August 2003.

13 *Manchester Evening News*, Friday 20 June 1952.

14 Paul Mason, memory sheet, 12 March 2000.

15 Jackie Kerr, memory sheet, 21 April 2003.

CHAPTER 6

TILES, STAINED GLASS & TURNSTILES:
THREE LOCAL FIRMS

For several years we tried to establish who made the wonderful tiles and the magnificent stained glass windows at Victoria Baths. The libraries were scoured for information, visits made to the Whitworth Art Gallery and other places further afield to see if they could help. All to no avail, and the Council said they had no record.

At last we solved both questions. In 2002, for the first time, one of the green tiles came loose from the wall of the entrance hall. Treating it with utmost respect we looked at the back for marks – it is marked BURTONS PATENT with a Registered Design number 380753 and two Ps in the corners. We could not interpret this ourselves but a few phone calls soon led to an answer – the tiles were made by the Pilkington's Tile Company.[1]

The Pilkingtons of Lancashire were colliery owners, owning the Clifton and Kearsley Colliery Co.

Tiles at Victoria Baths, the predominant tile (left) was made by Pilkington's.

CHAPTER 6

This raised more questions: how did Pilkingtons Colliery Co. become tile makers? It came about by a sequence of events which started in 1888 when mining shafts were being sunk at Clifton Junction, a small village between Manchester and Bolton. During the work large quantities of red marl were found and it was thought this might be suitable for making bricks. Advice was sought by James Lee Wood, Secretary of the Clifton and Kearsley company, from one William Burton. Wood had met Burton at Owen's College, (the precursor of Manchester University), where the latter, a chemist at Josiah Wedgwood & Sons, lectured. There is a postcard at the factory from Wood to Burton recalling their earlier acquaintance and opening the discussion about the clay.[2]

The clay was found to be unsuitable for brick-making, but Burton suggested they consider the production of ceramic tiles for which there was a strong demand. The idea was attractive to the Pilkingtons who were interested in artistic matters, and also concerned to provide employment for the wives of their coalminers. Tile making was a job mainly for women. So in 1891 a new company was incorporated under the name Pilkington's Pottery Co. Ltd.

Frederick C. Howells who designed the green tile used at Victoria Baths.

The Pilkingtons offered Burton the job of manager of the new company and he was given command of the whole project. Because he was under contract to Wedgwood, Burton was unable to start work with Pilkingtons until late 1892, but in the meantime persuaded the company to employ his younger brother, Joseph, who thus became its first employee in December 1891. Joseph too played a major role in Pilkingtons, eventually succeeding William as company manager in 1915.

From 1892 the name of the company was changed to Pilkington's Tile and Pottery Co. Ltd. It was a happy and rewarding time. Under William Burton's expert leadership the new factory was built and a small group of key workers was brought in, many of them from Stoke. The new factory developed into a major tile producer and generated profits almost continuously during Burton's time there.

William Burton had a remarkable ability to recognise and attract artistic talent. Well-known designers were commissioned to provide designs, firstly for tiles and later for pottery. He encouraged the production of decorative tiles, with Persian-style ones being made for a long period. Some of these were supplied for the ill-fated *Titanic*.

Besides using artists working on commission, Burton was concerned to recruit employees with artistic ability. A growing team of direct employees became involved, one of whom was Frederick C. Howells, who designed our Victoria Baths tiles. His work is mentioned in the catalogue of the Wolverhampton Exhibition of 1902 with an illustration of his tiles, described in the catalogue as 'Embossed tiles in coloured glazes for dados, wall-fillings etc. designed by F C Howells'. Burton had recognised his worth as a tile draughtsman and had written to him concerning his employment with the company. The factory has this letter, dated 2 December 1895, confirming the appointment of Howells, written in William Burton's own beautiful flowing handwriting. A new department, with its own draughtsmen, was formed under Howells' leadership to handle large-scale tiling jobs.[3] Victoria Baths was one of these. Little else is known of Howells's work as a designer and the tiles at Victoria Baths may be one of very few of his designs that were produced. Howells left Pilkington's to work for Craven Dunnill in Shropshire in 1916, again working in production rather than design.

The enduring success of Howells' work is reflected in the memories recorded by many of our visitors. One lady writes of the beautiful ornamentation of the tiles 'It felt so luxurious to be wrapped in a towel amid the beauty of this building'.[4] Another visitor who remembers taking part in school galas at Victoria Baths before her family moved to Kenya says:

> Coming back after 47 years, it would have been devastating to see the state of this beautiful building as it is now, without the knowledge that so many 'Friends' are determined to get it up and running again. It will be worth it for the green and cream tiles alone! A marvellous building.[5]

Another lady writes of her memories of Victoria Baths when she was 8 years old: 'Even at that age, I was fascinated by the building. I spent more time examining the interior design and décor than I did swimming.'[6]

So the story of our Pilkington tiles, the work of William Burton and Frederick Howells lives on, and it is a wonderful bonus to have at last gained this insight as to how it all began.

The Stained Glass

In 2002, after being boarded over for some ten years, the stained glass windows of the frontage of Victoria Baths were revealed in all their rich Art Nouveau glory. As part of the 'Urgent Works' programme undertaken that year, these windows were protected by clear, reinforced plastic. The sunlight streaming through their vibrant colours gives a breathtaking glimpse of the artistry of the Victorian glassmakers and also threw light on another mystery – who made these marvellous windows?

As a result of some lovely colour photographs taken by David Montford in 1975 and published in the *Manchester Evening News* and the *Manchester Metro News* to advertise our first Open Day of 2003, along with a request for information about the makers of the stained glass, there were many phone calls to the office. One caller left a very straightforward message: 'I can tell you who made those windows, it was my Great Uncle, William Pointer.'[7]

during a demonstration of a submarine in the water and his diminutive size meant he became known as 'the little Robin', later abbreviated to 'Rob'. The name stuck for the rest of his life.

Recognised as the fleetest of British sprinters from 1897 until 1907 when he became the first Englishman to break 1 minute for 100 yards freestyle, his speed was a great asset to the Manchester Osborne Swimming Club water polo team whom he played for. At the 1900 Olympics in Paris the

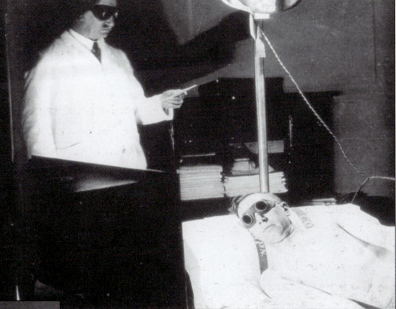

Top: A customer undergoing Sun Ray treatment.
Left: Mr Botham, Superintendent of Victoria Baths 1945-60, watching his daughter Jean, 1957.

Manchester Osborne team won the gold medal in the first Olympic water polo competition. Rob was capped nine times during 1896,1898, 1899 (captain) and in 1900, and was in the Manchester team which won the national water polo competition on seven occasions.[4] His father must have been very proud of Rob's achievements.

Mr Derbyshire was followed as General Superintendent by Mr Albert Teasdale. He oversaw many improvements and modernisations to Victoria Baths including new procedures for water treatment. Another innovation in his time was the opening at Victoria Baths of an Artificial Sun Ray Department, open to men and women six days a week, under the care of skilled men and women operators. Every person desiring treatment would undergo a test given

Crown Green Bowls became popular in the 1950s, played when the First Class Pool was boarded over for the winter months.

by an operator who, upon the results of the test, decided the length of exposure that could be applied with beneficial results and without the risks of ill effects.[5]

Mr Teasdale gave his swimmers all his support and encouragement, ably assisted by his daughter, Muriel. In those years of strict amateur rules, she attended many staff meetings, and fought to get good price concessions from Bukta on the swimming costumes for her club members. As we have seen in Zilpha Grant's story, she had many reasons to be grateful for Muriel Teasdale's help and support. Muriel and Mrs Teasdale are also remembered for giving Christmas parties for the children at Victoria Baths.[6]

Mr Frank Botham worked as General Superintendent from 1945 to 1960 and continued the good work set by his predecessors, encouraging all his visitors to enjoy safely their swimming and other activities at Victoria Baths. He kept the annual galas going and made the dance nights ever more popular. The boarding over of the Gala Pool during the winter months made this area the venue for all

Jean Botham (above) and Doreen Pollitt on the steps of Victoria Baths, 1952.

the important crown green bowls matches and a welcome source of income for the Baths and Laundries Committee.

In 1957 the annual income from the bowling at Victoria Baths stood at £202 4s. 8d. This dropped slightly in the following years due to periods of closure because of painting and maintenance work.[7]

A Council report states:

From the winter season of 1958-59, after the Committee had organised a challenge competition for indoor Crown Green Bowls with 6-a-side teams taking part, the takings started to rise again. 66 teams entered and considerable interest was aroused and retained throughout the contest. It is hoped that as a result of this innovation the bowls clubs themselves will run their own future competitions.[8]

Another innovation during Mr Botham's career was the installation of the Therapeutic Aeratone Bath

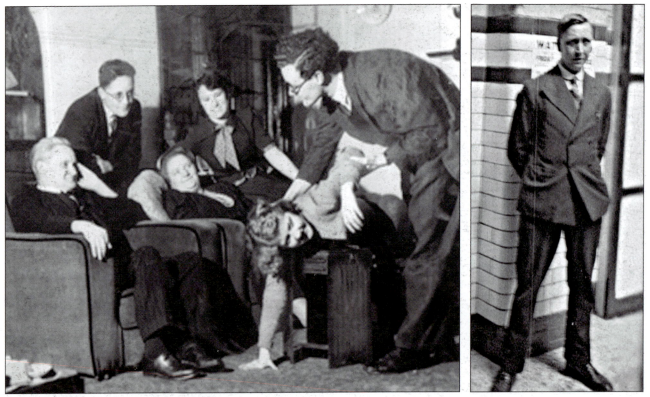

Left: The Botham family in the Superintendent's Flat, 1949; Jean is being coached by her brother Roy.
Right: Harry Williams who worked as a fireman and then a foreman at Victoria Baths, 1918-33.

at Victoria Baths in 1952, the first of its kind in England.[9] It became very popular with the general public and also much appreciated by the medical profession. The doctors at Manchester Royal Infirmary would often refer their patients to have an Aeratone Bath at Victoria.

There were four children in the Botham family: Roy, Ella, William (Bill) and Jean. They were all good swimmers, as one would expect. It must have been wonderful, almost as if they had their own private swimming pools at home. They certainly benefited from all the after-hours training they were able to enjoy. One of Jean Botham's friends writes: 'I used to swim with Jean Botham after the Baths had closed. With her living there we would swim all night sometimes till her Mum or Dad came to make us get out of the pool.'[10]

Roy, Botham's eldest son, swam in the 1948 Olympics in London and also in the 1952 Olympics in Helsinki. Jean Botham, the youngest in the family, also competed in the 1952 Olympics, when Jean and Roy were the first brother and sister to swim in the same Olympic Games.[11] Roy and Jean also took part in many other national and international events and Roy in water polo matches.

Above: The Committee Room was used to entertain senior swimmers and important guests following swimming galas, this being such an occasion in 1973 (photo: David Montford).
Right: Detail of the frieze, 1906.

Bill Botham is remembered by many for his skills and dedication to the South Manchester Water Polo team. A member of the team writes about 'the unforgettable Bill Botham (son of Mr F. R. Botham) who lived at Victoria Baths for much of his early days and gave so freely of his time and enthused so many swimmers and polo players.'[12]

It is clear that the superintendents of Victoria Baths and their families played a very important part in the swimming history of Manchester. When Mr Botham retired in 1960, the Baths Committee offered the position of General Superintendent at Victoria Baths to Mr Harry Hitchin. He and his family were then living in London and it was not until January 1961 that they were able to move into their flat at the Baths. Iris Hitchin records that

CHAPTER 7

I remember arriving at Victoria Baths in January 1961. The beautiful building was bathed in sunshine, and the children were saying, 'Are we going to live here? Wow!' There was a wooden plaque on the front door, with 'Victoria House' picked out in gold lettering. We later received letters addressed to Mr & Mrs Hitchin, Victoria House, Manchester, so it was well known. Mrs Botham came to tell me that a man came to wind the clock each Thursday morning. He also came late on a Saturday in the Spring and Autumn to change the time. The hands of the clock were set at 12 o/c, according to the Byelaws at the time on Public Clocks. Access was through our flat when the clock stopped. We could only hear the mechanism of the clock and a thump on every hour, never the clock chiming. The Gala Pool was converted into a hall in the Winter and used for Crown Green bowling. Later, badminton and five-a-side football were introduced and the Sauna Bath installed.

Fyffe Robertson recorded a programme for the BBC and shipwreck scenes for the making of a programme on the sinking of the *Titanic*. Some of the staff were used as extras for these scenes. Miss Nugent from *Coronation Street* presented prizes at some of our school Galas. Scenes with Hilda Ogden were filmed outside the building. A flagpole in the forecourt was blown down in high winds in the mid-60s. Until then the Union Jack was always flown on important dates, St George's Day, Royal Birthdays, Commonwealth Day, etc. The square stone with a hole in the centre, into which the Flagpole used to be inserted, is still visible, in situation in the forecourt. The Manchester Schools Championships were held annually at Victoria and the officials and members of the Baths Committee, met in the Committee Room for refreshments. Once a month the Royal Life Saving Society held their meetings there. Training Sessions for the North West (Amateur) Swimming Association were held in all three pools, once a fortnight.[13]

Mr and Mrs Hitchin returned to Victoria Baths in October 2003 and were given a tour of the building including, of course, the flat which they had left in August 1972 when Mr Hitchin retired. Mrs Hitchin said she had so many happy memories which came flooding back when she saw her flat. She tells me that it has taken her a long time to get used to living in an ordinary house, away from Victoria Baths, and still misses it. Mrs Hitchin wrote: 'Our return to "Victoria" was quite an emotional one for me, it brought back so many memories. It was lovely to meet so many people who have worked so hard to restore the Baths, and we wish you every success.'[13]

There were, of course, many other workers at Victoria Baths as well as the Superintendent; from the towel boys in the Turkish Baths to the much-respected swimming teachers and coaches.

The Laverty family, Jack and his daughters Nellie and Marion became famous as swimming teachers and coaches at Victoria Baths in the 1920s. In fact Jack Laverty had already started his career as coach and trainer under the auspices of Mr Derbyshire. For the 1930 Empire Games in Hamilton, Ontario, Nellie Laverty trained Miss Cecilia Wolstenholme, who came first, and Miss Margery Hinton, second, in the Women's breaststroke event.[14]

Another of my correspondents, now in his nineties, also recalls Cecilia's great win. He also mentions Joe Whiteside as being English 100 yards backstroke champion.[15] He would have been trained by Jack Laverty in those days of strict segregation of the sexes.

I have also had lots of stories about Arthur Howarth. He was born in 1921 in City Road, Manchester, in the flat above his Grandma's cookshop. He joined the Navy and did twelve years service in the Royal Marines. He was a good, stylish swimmer and gained awards in the Service teams. After his demob, he

CHAPTER 7

was advised to apply for the position of swimming teacher for Manchester Education Committee. He did, and got the job at Victoria Baths. There he taught school children for some thirty years, mainly in the Second Class Males Pool, later referred to as the 'No. 2 Pool'.

Many of our visitors, who were taught by Mr Howarth, speak fondly of their school swimming lessons. He was able to give the children the confidence they needed, telling them to hold on to the side until they felt ready to try a few strokes. He always told them the more confidence they had, the better swimmers they would become.

A gentleman writes of being taught by Mr Howarth and being proud to become winner of the Howarth Trophy. He says, 'I still have that medal to this day. That man was an inspiration. So much so that I went on to become the first British disabled swimmer of the English Channel. I owe him an enormous debt'.[16] Barbara Gordon writes:

Arthur was Manchester Education Committee Swimming Teacher for local schools, private schools and play centres. He taught some 2,000 children a week from 9am to 4pm, 40 per class. There were Galas every year and his children had extra training to take part. One remembers the stars coming [to use the Turkish Baths], Tommy Cooper, Dennis Law, Bobby Charlton. Arthur would ask for their autographs so that he could give them to the children as incentive to further effort.

When teaching the very little ones, he would tell them to hold on to one another and walk along the shallow end, while singing 'We all live in a yellow submarine'. On 'submarine' they would all duck. This overcame their fear and made swimming fun.

Arthur received a Certificate from Lord Mountbatten for services teaching lifesaving.

Needless to say, he enjoyed every minute of working at Victoria Baths. When he retired after 30 years service, he was given a 'leaving do' at St Joseph's School. He has recently been awarded the M.B.E. for Life Saving.[17]

I am very grateful to Margaret Jump, who has provided a very comprehensive account of her father and mother's involvement with Victoria Baths. She records:

My father, Robert Henry Williams, known by everybody as Harry Williams, worked at Victoria after he came home from the war in 1918. He had been a soldier in the Manchester Regiment; he served in France and was a prisoner of war in Germany. He never spoke of these experiences to us. He had a good friend from these early days, a Mr Lionel Pate, who also became a Baths Manager.

On his return from the war he met my mother – her story was that he had spent his gratuity money and was hard up! He would be about 21-22 years old, when he worked as a fireman at Victoria and he continued to work there until 1933 – he worked his way up, becoming foreman and later, I understand, a management position, the photograph in a smart suit, taken with Mr Teasdale, proves this.

My mother came from Longsight, her name was Hilda Fisher. She joined the staff at Victoria Baths and worked in various areas, the wash baths, the Turkish Baths and later as office staff.. They became an 'item' as they say today and married on Saturday, August 29th 1925. My mother had to retire from work, as married women did not continue work in those days.

My father got promotion to Cheetham Baths as a manager and later, in 1941, was promoted to Levenshulme Baths by

CHAPTER 7

Mr Botham. This had very pleasant living accommodation.

Despite the worry of the war, with air raids, rationing and shortages, we were happy in our new life, but sadness came with the death of my brother, Robert, he was only 16.

My father took up bowling, he became Secretary of Levenshulme Bowling Club. Dad loved life, his family, and his work, his hobbies and Manchester City. He was a man's man, and unfortunately had smoked heavily all his life. He died in November 1955 after a short illness. I never recall him being off work and to lose him so suddenly was a great sadness.

He had been so conscientious to his work as Manager. He had achieved this status from such humble beginnings – no Grammar School, no University, no management studies, so different from today. I am so proud of his achievement.

My own wedding was planned for June 1956 and sadly Mum and I had to leave Levenshulme even before that date, not only had my mother lost her husband, but also her home. She was only 53.

Mr Johnstone, who worked for the Baths Department suggested, to help her grief, she go back to work at the Laundry and this she did, and guess where she worked? Yes, Victoria Baths! It was hard work, but the group of ladies she worked with were a jolly crowd (one was a German lady called Gerda).

My own sons were born in 1957 and 1963 and we moved to Cheltenham in 1965. I encouraged my mother to join us there. Eventually she had a 'Granny flat' built on to my house for her final years.

Mum managed her life with great dignity, her priority was her home and family, she never owed a penny to anyone. I am so proud of both my parents.

To conclude I must relate that they too would have been proud to know that my dear little Grandson, now aged 5, is called Robert.[18]

As an appendix to Robert Henry Williams's story, I can't resist adding a short item sent to me by Mr Pate's daughter, Mary Britten.

Mr Lionel A. Pate started work in Victoria Baths in 1909 as a towel boy in the Turkish Baths. He served in the First World War with the 2nd Manchester Pals and was voted the smartest soldier in the British Army (a joint win for which he then lost the prize on the toss of a coin!).

Apart from his years in the Army, Mr Pate worked at Victoria Baths for 22 years until he was promoted to manage several baths and wash-houses – Moss Side, Withington, Newton Heath and, in 1937, Mayfield.[19] A letter of reference written by Mr Teasdale in 1929 reflects very highly on Mr Pate and also Victoria Baths – 'the largest and most important Establishment in this City.'

When the war started, Mary was evacuated because Mayfield Baths was considered to be in a very dangerous position, near to London Road station, the Dunlop rubber factory, and other firms doing important war work. She came home to Mayfield Baths for Christmas and brought a chicken for the family dinner from the farmer.

She says:

You never hear the bomb that lands near you, the first I knew of it was me flying across the room, and although there were thick blackout blinds on the window, I saw it crack from top to bottom and my chicken flying through the window. Dad went out to retrieve it. He decided things were getting too hot, so he moved us from the Baths shelter, down underground into a large sewer pipe which ran under the street between the Baths and the Wash-house, it was

Lionel Pate who worked at Victoria Baths for 22 years.

quite dry. After the 'all clear', we emerged from our shelter to see the devastation all around us, everything was badly damaged and Mayfield Wash-house was unusable. The local people relied on our Wash-house. The nearest laundry was at Victoria Baths so that was opened to the general public, so that they could have at least clean clothes and sheets for their beds.[20]

The engineers and boiler house maintenance workers were very important people. On them depended the daily smooth running of baths and wash-houses, where so much heat was needed for the swimming baths, Turkish baths, wash baths and laundries.

One such was Jack Turner, who worked at Victoria Baths from 1960 to 1985. When he first arrived there, after the lean war years, he often had to travel to Wales and Birmingham to buy old washing machines and spare parts for the laundry, which he could then restore. He also bought lathes, milling machines and tools to equip his workshop.

He writes:

I was a center lathe turner, and I worked at Victoria Baths for over 20 years. I was supervisor of the workshop. When I first started I had a workshop in the old Boiler House. My first job was to make new square threads for the Lancashire Boiler they had not been changed for donkeys' years and were almost stripped of all threads. Later I had a workshop to the right hand side of the laundry and also an extra room in what had been the canteen next to the laundry.[21]

This had become necessary, as Jack by now had several apprentice engineers, helping to maintain all the machinery. He tells me that he did have a photo of his well-equipped workshop, of which he was very proud, but it was taken to be filed in Manchester Town Hall before he managed to get a copy.

This pride in their work comes through very forcibly when I read through the memories people have of their time at the High Street Baths. They express their happiness at work, and also the pride they feel in the jobs well done.

Baths Department Day Trip.

One gentleman writes:

I started work in Manchester on leaving the Army in December 1957. I was classed as a trainee manager. In 1959 I was working at Pryme Street Wash-house as a stoker and I was summoned to the City Hall to meet the 'infamous' Frank Botham. My knees were knocking, but I was delighted to find I was not in trouble. I was being promoted to be a stoker at Victoria Baths. I was over the moon, because that was where all the potential Managers finished their training.

Going to the High Street was like going to Mars. The size of the plant – 2 large boilers, an economiser and the defunct steam driven pumping system from what I was told was an artesian well to feed the pools – it was just another world. I was so proud. I learnt so much under Mr Botham's senior staff that when the new Wythenshawe (Sharston) pool opened, Mr Botham transferred me to be an Assistant Manager. On one hand I was delighted and on the other I was sad because I was leaving an old friend.

The 2 years I spent at Victoria Baths were the happiest times in my career.

Now retired, I miss Victoria Baths, and I still see the customers and the staff as if it were yesterday.[22]

CHAPTER 7

Notes

1 Jean Jensen, née Botham, e-mail, 4 July 2003.

2 Ernie Ivor Derbyshire, telephone call, October 2003

3 Mrs E. Ridyard, memory sheet, 2 March 2003.

4 Dr Ian Gordon's notes on swimming.

5 *How Manchester is Managed* (1930), pp. 38-41.

6 Mrs Parkinson, née Thatcher, memory sheet, 30 June 2001.

7 Manchester Baths and Laundries Committee Report 1962, p. 22.

8 Manchester Baths and Laundries Committee Report 1958-59, pp. 14, 16.

9 *Manchester Evening News*, 20 June 1952.

10 Doreen Thompson, née Pollitt, telephone calls, 2003.

11 Sarah Bryant, e-mail, 5 May 2003.

12 Mike Kirkman, e-mail, 6 April 2003.

13 Mrs Iris Hitchin, memory sheets, 31 January 2004.

14 *Manchester Evening News*, 19 August 1930.

15 J. Mottershead, memory sheet, December 2001.

16 Mike Cooke, e-mail, 23 September 2003.

17 Barbara Gordon, memory sheet, 15 September 2003 and phone call 12 January 2004.

18 Margaret Jump, letter, June 2002.

19 Newspaper cutting announcing Mr Pate's retirement.

20 Mrs M. Britten, née Pate, memory sheet, 2 October 2003.

21 Jack Turner, letters 24, 30 September 2002, also phone call 10 November 2002.

22 Donald Muirhead, e-mail, 22 September 2003.

CHAPTER 8

DANCE NIGHTS, FILM & OTHER USES

It may have been dark and freezing cold outside Victoria Baths, but once you made your way through the sumptuous entrance hall and heard the welcoming strains of the dance music played by the Big Bands of Percy Pease, Phil Moss, Ted Heath or other well-known band-leaders, you knew with a flutter of excitement, that you were in for an evening of unrivalled enjoyment.

The Gala Pool, boarded over for the winter months, would be suitably embellished with floral baskets and greenery, and the stage was well-lit, now occupied by the smartly dressed musicians. The music was not too overpowering, and it was possible to converse easily with one's partner while enjoying the dancing. It is the music which lives on in the memories of so many who still recall the haunting melodies of the '30s, '40s and '50s – the never to be forgotten *Shine on Harvest Moon*, *Ramona*, *You Made Me Love You* and, of course, *In The Mood*.

Dancing has long been a favourite pastime, a ball, an occasion for dressing up and looking one's best, but for so long it had been the prerogative of the few. In the Manchester area it had become the custom to hold balls at venues such as town halls or public halls, but the hire of these large rooms was expensive, and then there were the musicians' fees too. Admission charges had to be high, so balls were beyond the reach of most of the working population. In the 1920s the hire of Manchester Town Hall's large room for holding a ball for over three hours was £75. At the Free Trade Hall the cost was similar. There were cheaper venues ranging from Hulme Town Hall at £10 10s. 0d, down to the bargain price at Withington Town Hall of £3 15s. 0d.[1]

But things were improving, a dance evening was becoming increasingly affordable to more young people. By the early 1930s people were going to dances at such venues as church halls and football clubs. Any pub or club which had a hall of any size ran its own dances. Not to be outdone, the Manchester Baths and Wash-houses Committee decided that after the main swimming season ended, the pools at certain baths could be boarded over to be used as public halls for concerts and dances from the second week in October to the second week in April. This proved to be a valuable source of income for the Committee, rising steadily from £580 in 1939, when only four pools were boarded over, to £1,583 12s. 6d in 1948-9.[2]

The popularity of dance nights at Victoria Baths lives on in the memories of all who danced, waltzed and later jived on the boards covering the empty pool. Mrs Kath Bethell tells of her very happy memories of the dance nights:

During the Dance season, I would go every Saturday night. We used to dance to the music of Percy Pease and his Band, to the tunes of *Moonlight Serenade, The Old Lamplighter, Come Back to Sorrento, In The Mood*. The Christmas Eve and New Year's Eve Dances were magic. There was a good, happy atmosphere, no alcohol was served, only soft drinks, tea and coffee, cakes and biscuits. I used to go with my sister and friends and we would sit with a crowd of boys who played for a local soccer team called Fallowfield Rangers. When the evening was over we used to walk home to Old Trafford.

I have very special, affectionate memories of High Street Baths Dance, because it was there I met my husband Alan, in January 1947. He was in the army and home on leave from Malta. We have now been happily married 45 years.[3]

A visitor to one of our Open Days in September 1999 wrote of 'The Floor that served the dancing'. She too has fond memories of the High Street dance nights. She says they had lots of fun dancing to the music of Percy Pease and his Band. Percy would ask, 'Has everybody bought their costume?'

She also recalls that Phil Moss was a member of Percy Pease's Band before he formed his own in the 1940s.[4] Increasingly it was his music to which people danced each Saturday night at Victoria Baths Ballroom. He introduced new features, including 'Dancing in the Dark' which is often referred to by our

The First Class Pool was boarded over from October to April.

visitors. One lady remembers:

> I never learnt to swim, but I came to the dances. I remember especially the 'Dancing in the Dark'. The Band had parts of their clothing which was fluorescent and showed up when the lights were dimmed.[5]

There is a lovely description of this feature in Phil Moss's recent book, *True Romances of Manchester Dances*, in which Ellen Metcalf recalls:

> I loved the Dancing in the Dark spot, the lights going out and the fluorescent light taking over, picking out the white shirts and dresses and making everything glow. The singer would dance, or rather glide, across the stage to the music and the whole effect was quite spectacular. It really was the highlight of the evening.[6]

Phil would introduce guest singers. Frankie Vaughan, Dicky Valentine, Joan Savage and Ronnie Hilton are often mentioned by our visitors when talking about the dance nights. Phil would also play special requests for jivers who would all go to one end of the dance floor, where they would jive to the inspiring music to their heart's content.[7]

Albert Smith wrote after seeing a letter of mine in the *Manchester Evening News*. He said, 'I am writing to say my abiding memory of the High Street Baths is the dancing, where I spent many happy hours dancing to the music of the Phil Moss Dance Band.'[8] Albert has recently told me more of his story. He learnt to dance at Cowan's in Moss Side before joining the Parachute Regiment and serving overseas during the war. He was demobbed in 1948 and returned to his job at Pike's Bakery on Hyde Road, near Belle Vue. He wasted no time and was busy renewing old acquaintances and re-visiting the places he had missed during the war. He decided to go dancing at Cowan's but met one of his pals, Jimmy Atkinson, who had a date at High Street Baths, so he tossed a coin and went to High Street with Jimmy.

There he met a beautiful blonde who came over and said 'Don't you work at the Pike's Bakery?' He said he did and realised he had seen her occasionally at work. Her name was Eleanor May Westwood. They danced together and this chance meeting was the start of their life-long romance. They were married in March 1950 and had twin boys, now in their fifties. Their sons were always eager to hear stories of their parents' romantic meeting.

Sadly, Eleanor died in 2001 and Albert is now busy writing up his memories of his eventful life. He says that this has helped him to come to terms with life without Eleanor. He also enjoys listening to his CDs of classical and Big Band music. Albert says, 'If you cannot dance, it leaves you with a big hole in your life'. The High Street Dance Nights and the Phil Moss Band played a very important part in his life.[9]

Another romance which started at a High Street Baths dance night is even more intriguing. It began as a 'blind date' on 8 February 1947. Beatrice Hooley had arranged to go to the dance at the High Street Baths with her friend, Mary. Mary was coming with her soldier-boyfriend, a military policeman, who

Beatrice Hooley and Bill Ramsden who met on a 'blind date' at a Victoria Baths dance night.

was bringing his friend, Bill Ramsden, to meet Beatrice. As it turned out, Mary's boyfriend couldn't come as he was on duty, so only Bill came. He, too, was a tall, handsome military policeman, and when he and Beatrice met, it was love at first sight. The evening whirled by as they danced to the romantic strains of the Phil Moss Band, but, like Cinderella, Beatrice had to leave in a rush. She had to be home at 10 o'clock as her father was a very strict, almost Victorian, disciplinarian. He tried, but failed, to stop Bill and Beatrice meeting, but their romance blossomed. Bill was shortly demobbed and immediately proposed marriage, but they faced a very difficult situation. The strict father would not give his permission, which they needed as Beatrice was only eighteen.[10] To try to force his consent, they decided to tell him of the baby on the way but it didn't work. A furious father threw Beatrice out despite her mother's pleading.

Bill took her to his parents in Yorkshire where she was made very welcome and it all ended happily. They applied to the court for permission to marry and the hearing came up on 8 June. It was a very long

CHAPTER 8

Another romance which began at Victoria Baths – Marjory and Ray Waterhouse in the dance hall at Victoria Baths.

day for them as they were last on the list of applicants. At 4 o'clock they were called in and five minutes later they were told they had the court's permission. A weight was lifted from their shoulders and they celebrated at a local café, with tea and cakes.

Bill went to see the vicar on 10 June, and the wedding, with homemade cake, took place on 12 June 1947 at 8 o'clock in the morning. Bill had asked the vicar for the earliest possible time. After all their troubles he didn't want to wait a minute longer than necessary. Their baby, a lovely boy, Russell, was born in November. Bill, now working, was able to provide for them and they soon moved to their own home. They had their second child, a girl, Cheryl, 3 years later. Cheryl now lives in California, and Bill and Beatrice visited on several occasions to see her and her two daughters, Justine and Stephanie. Beatrice says her grandchildren always wanted to hear all about her romantic story of meeting grandad on a 'blind date' at Victoria Baths dance on a bleak February evening.

Sadly, Beatrice is now widowed, but she has three grandchildren and three great-grandchildren. She

CHAPTER 8

speaks fondly of her family and is so happy and proud to have brought up such a loving, caring family. She also speaks fondly of her memories of Victoria Baths dance nights, where it all began.[11]

Eventually, and sadly, the regular dance nights at Victoria Baths came to an end. Phil Moss and his Band moved to the Ritz in Whitworth Street and many devotees of his music followed him there. Other dance venues sprang up to cater for the more affluent young people of the 1970s and '80s. However, Victoria Baths was not forgotten and it worked its magic once again in 1989, not as a boarded-over dance floor but as a venue for a 'Pool Party' and demonstration of Aqua Aerobics. Suzanne Fenby writes:

> There was a pool party, Hacienda style, hosted by Anthony Wilson. It was shown on Granada TV. People who normally went to the Hacienda were here. There was music (DJs), lighting, etc just like the Hacienda, but everyone was in their swimming costume. I think it was an extension of the H.O.T. night at the Hacienda, where there was a small pool at the club. Well, here the main pool was open and all the Turkish Baths facilities. I saw it as an opportunity to see Victoria Baths in all its glory; its future was in doubt at this time.
> There was also Aqua Aerobics on this night which was a bit of a laugh as at this time no one had seen it before.[12]

It may be the exuberant beauty and grandeur of our Baths which has inspired many stars from the world of entertainment to visit and perform some of their best work here. Victoria Baths has been used as the backdrop for the TV film, *Prime Suspect Five* starring Helen Mirren. Fyffe Robertson recorded a programme for the BBC and shipwreck scenes for the making of a programme on the sinking of the *Titanic*. Some of the staff were used as extras for these scenes.

Scenes for *Coronation Street* with Hilda Ogden were filmed outside the building. There was also the filming here of one of his programmes by the well-known psychic, Derek Acorah, now best known for his TV show *Most Haunted*. His findings here were, to say the least, surprising!

But it is the Bee Gees, and especially Barry Gibb, who hold a special place in the hearts of all at Victoria Baths. For it was here that Barry made his feature length video, *Now Voyager*, which was planned for release in conjunction with his first solo album in 1984. Barry said, 'It's something I've always wanted to do.' He co-wrote most of the songs with George Bitzer, a very fine pianist, some with his brother Maurice and one with Robin.

Now Voyager was named after one of Barry's favourite films, starring Bette Davis, although the album has nothing to do with the 1942 classic. There was no *Now Voyager* song on his album, although an instrumental item, written by Barry, called *Theme From Now Voyager* is heard on the video. This has a storyline loosely connecting most of the songs.

Barry, the chief actor in the drama, is plunged into limbo and made to reflect on his life which is shown though the songs. Playing the role of part conscience/part guardian angel was the distinguished British actor, Sir Michael Hordern. The stunning backdrop of Victoria Baths interior, with its many pools – 'three in fact', as Sir Michael Hordern tells Barry – plays an important part in the film. The Aeratone and the Turkish Baths are also featured.

CHAPTER 8

As a result of the *Now Voyager* video, Victoria Baths has received a number of visits from interested Bee Gees fans in recent years. They have come to Manchester to visit various Bee Gees-related sites, including the house in Chorlton where the brothers Gibb grew up.

Victoria Baths has continued to be used as a location for TV and film productions, including *Sherlock Holmes*, *Cracker* and *City Central*.

Notes
1 *Official Handbook Manchester and Salford* (1922), p. 111.
2 Manchester Baths & Wash-houses Reports.
3 Mrs Kath Bethell, memory sheet, 25 August 1999.
4 Mrs Doris Dawson, memory sheet, 12 September 1999.
5 Mrs P. Butterworth, memory sheet, 12 March 2000.
6 Phil Moss, *True Romances of Manchester Dances* (1998), p. 22.
7 Mr P. Gibson, letter, February 2002.
8 Albert Smith, card, 18 February 2002.
9 Albert Smith, telephone calls, 16 & 18 February 2003.
10 Beatrice Ramsden, memory sheet, 29 April 2001.
11 Beatrice Ramsden, telephone calls, February 2003.
12 Suzanne Fenby, memory sheet, 10 March 2001.

CHAPTER 9

CLOSURE, THE CAMPAIGN & THE FUTURE

Gill Wright

Victoria Baths was closed for public use on 13 March 1993. There had been just a couple of months warning of the closure, enough time, though, for a vigorous campaign to build up amongst local residents. Whilst the numbers of people swimming at Victoria Baths had declined over the years, those who did swim there really appreciated the local facility. And the Turkish Baths, Aeratone and dry sports facilities were still well used. Local people also recognised that Victoria Baths was a very significant building architecturally. They were determined that it should not be lost. Following requests from the campaigners, supported by the local M.P., Gerald Kaufman, English Heritage reconsidered the listed status of Victoria Baths, and it was upgraded to Grade II★ on the list of Buildings of Architectural and Historic Interest.

By March 1993 Victoria Baths needed at least £500,000 spending on the building and plant for it to remain operational. The City Council felt it could not justify this expense and it quickly became clear that closure was inevitable, despite a petition to the council signed by 16,000 people, demonstrations and a 'Dry Swim' held in Albert Square in front of the Town Hall. So the local campaigners looked at ways of raising money independently to carry out the work needed to restore Victoria Baths. With advice from the Architectural Heritage Fund, a building preservation trust – the Victoria Baths Trust – was set up in August 1993 and registered as a charity. The wider, campaigning body was constituted as the Friends of Victoria Baths. The Trust and the Friends have the same aim – to restore and re-open for public use at least one of the swimming pools at Victoria Baths and the Turkish Baths.

In the years since 1993 the Trust has received support from a number of grant-giving bodies in its endeavours to draw up a viable plan for the restoration of Victoria Baths. Most importantly it has received support from the Architectural Heritage Fund and English Heritage. The Architectural Heritage Fund has provided grant aid towards a feasibility study and a development study as well as very valuable advice and support. English Heritage was the first body to provide a capital grant for Victoria Baths when they supported a programme of emergency work to the building in 2002. This enabled the Trust to commission crucial holding work to the building – patching roofs, dealing with dry rot and providing for ventilation. The work was also funded by the A6 Corridor SRB Partnership.

In 2000 the Trust made applications to the Heritage Lottery Fund and the New Opportunities Fund for grant aid to restore Victoria Baths as a Healthy Living Centre. They were joined in this bid by another local charity (Diverse Resources), the City Council, as owners of the building, and the local Primary Care Trust. It was felt that the Healthy Living Centre was not only a very suitable use for the building, but it would be highly beneficial to the local community. The population surrounding the Baths has many health and social problems.

Both lottery bids were rejected, however, on the grounds that the Healthy Living Centre was not seen to be financially sustainable. This was in summer 2002 and was a great blow to the Trust and the Friends who had been working towards the Healthy Living Centre since 1998. But the campaigners, having been working towards saving Victoria Baths for over nine years, were not going to give up. Discussions were held with the City Council, the Heritage Lottery Fund and English Heritage and it was agreed that more work should be done to find a viable plan for the restoration of the building. The Trust made further applications for grant aid, employed a part-time project manager and drew up a brief to be given to consultants.

Above: Victoria Baths getting ready to win the BBC *Restoration* competition.
Right: *Well loved* lit sign by Alison Kershaw.

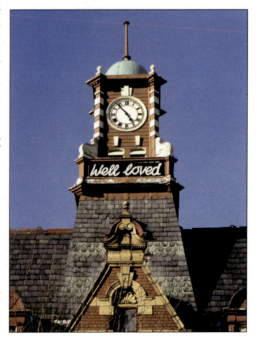

Then, along came BBC's *Restoration*! This ground-breaking series featured thirty listed buildings at risk from all over the UK. Each one of them had the potential to be restored for the benefit of the public and had a local group championing its cause. Presented with great passion by Griff Rhys Jones, the programme showed viewers the current state of each building and, through dramatic reconstructions, something of its history. We watched the Lord Mayor of Manchester opening Victoria Baths, Edwardian gentlemen steaming in the Turkish Baths, and young lads diving into the swimming pool. With over £3million on

Vote to Save

Victoria Baths

Manchester's 'Water Palace', the Victoria Baths is one of ten finalists in BBC2's Restoration. Everyone can vote and ONE building will receive over £3 million for its restoration. This is YOUR chance to save this beautiful, well loved building.

To vote for Victoria Baths ring

09010 77 50 01

Lines open from Thursday 11th Sep to 9.45pm on Sunday 14th Sep
The live final of Restoration is on BBC2 on Sunday 14th September at 9pm

＊ **You can vote as many times as you like** ＊
＊ Calls cost 30p of which 17.9p goes to the Restoration Fund ＊
Calls may cost more from a mobile
Note: Some mobile phones and some switchboards can't make this call

Victoria Baths is open for public view - see over for details

offer to the winner, viewers were invited to vote for the building they would most like to see restored.

By the summer of 2003 when *Restoration* was broadcast the Friends and the Trust were well used to working on the ground to raise awareness of their cause. Almost every year since closure they had opened the building at least twice to allow the public to look around, including on National Heritage Open Days. From 2000 the Trust had a formal agreement with Manchester City Council giving them day-to-day responsibility for providing access to the building and taking care of minor maintenance, etc. Volunteers from the Friends and Trust had carried out a great deal of minor work in the building – clearing out rubbish, cleaning up, providing basic amenities and putting up displays showing visitors something of the history of the Baths. In 2003 there were monthly Open Days, providing free guided tours of the building as well as the opportunity to share memories of the Baths, buy souvenirs and stop for a cup of tea. The Trust had also provided access to very many artists who were interested in the building as a starting point or setting for their work.

During the years they had been working to save Victoria Baths, the Trust and the Friends had built up a very wide network of supporters, not just the two hundred or so paid up members of the Friends, but a database of over five hundred contacts with interests ranging from health to historic pools, and installation art to ceramic tiles. Add to these the many thousands of people who have used Victoria Baths over the years and remember it well, and then add all those people who have never seen or heard of Victoria Baths but have fond memories of the baths where they learnt to swim which has since been demolished. When it came to the public vote the result was conclusive – the *nation* wanted to save Victoria Baths.

There were 282,018 votes for Victoria Baths, almost as many as the second and third building put together. The money secured as a result – £3 million from the Heritage Lottery Fund and £500,000 raised through the telephone vote and donations – will be used for the first stage of restoring the buildings, the reinstatement of the Turkish Baths for public use. It was a result which made very many people very happy, and not just the Friends and the Trust. As one ex-employee of Victoria Baths wrote: 'I am not ashamed to say that when you won the tears flowed and it made me realise what an important role that building had played in my life.'

The Trust is now working hard to turn the *Restoration* vote into a real restoration project, employing architects and other consultants to carry out all the necessary technical and planning work to enable the Turkish Baths at Victoria Baths to be restored to its former glory and re-opened for public use. Restoration work is due to begin on site at the end of 2005 and, if all goes to plan, the Turkish Baths will re-open to the public in 2007. The Trust is also working with its partners – Manchester City Council, English Heritage, the Heritage Lottery Fund, and the Restoration Fund – to establish how the remainder of the building can be restored. In particular we want to go on to achieve our other important objective, the reinstatement of one of the swimming pools for public use. This is a great challenge because swimming pools 'lose money' or 'require subsidy'. So any plan that is put forward for capital funding must show how this revenue deficit will be met.

CHAPTER 9

Victoria Baths was a controversial building project a hundred years ago. In a way history is being re-written. We live in hope that the foresight, vision and civic pride which gave the people of Manchester this marvellous building in 1906 will be repeated now and enable us once again to be very proud in Manchester of our 'Water Palace'.

INDEX

INDEX

INDEX

INDEX